Milena Bubenechik

The Trauma of Colonial Condition

in Nervous Conditions and Kiss of the Fur Queen

Anchor Academic
Publishing

Bubenechik, Milena: The Trauma of Colonial Condition: in Nervous Conditions and Kiss of the Fur Queen. Hamburg, Anchor Academic Publishing 2013

Buch-ISBN: 978-3-95489-087-3
PDF-eBook-ISBN: 978-3-95489-587-8
Druck/Herstellung: Anchor Academic Publishing, Hamburg, 2013

Bibliografische Information der Deutschen Nationalbibliothek:
Die Deutsche Nationalbibliothek verzeichnet diese Publikation in der Deutschen Nationalbibliografie; detaillierte bibliografische Daten sind im Internet über http://dnb.d-nb.de abrufbar.

Bibliographical Information of the German National Library:
The German National Library lists this publication in the German National Bibliography. Detailed bibliographic data can be found at: http://dnb.d-nb.de

© Anchor Academic Publishing, Imprint der Diplomica Verlag GmbH
Hermannstal 119k, 22119 Hamburg
http://www.diplomica-verlag.de, Hamburg 2013
Printed in Germany

Table of Contents

1. Introduction

This study will depict the traumatic condition of the formerly colonised indigenous peoples of Africa and Canada. The postcolonial trauma novels, Tomson Highway's *Kiss of the Fur Queen* (1998) and Tsitsi Dangarembga's *Nervous Conditions* (1988), are first-hand accounts of colonial experience under the governance of the British Empire of the second half of the twentieth century. The semi-autobiographical novels bring up the voices of the formerly silenced natives and are pioneering accounts of the native perception of Western intrusion. The narratives portray the upsetting experiences of the era of colonisation and explore the insidious consequences of living in the midst of historical change. The novels, written in English, speak back to the canon and expose the suffering of its subjects. They depict the grim atmosphere of the colonial project and show the effects of the domination, oppression, diaspora and discrimination suffered by the natives. The novels are life narratives and as such reveal facts not recorded in history books. The trauma novels enrich and challenge the discourse on (post)colonial trauma. The native authors, Dangarembga and Highway, explore the questions of identity, trauma and resistance in the context of colonization. Their approach queries traditional notions of identity formation and the common understanding of trauma and trauma healing. With their portrayal of unique means for resistance and survival, the novelists offer a challenge to the existing beliefs and theories.

In the study of the novels *Nervous Conditions* and *Kiss of the Fur Queen*, which allow silenced, repressed individuals to speak out about the unspeakable events of their lives, I will explore the formation of colonial and postcolonial identities, the nature and impact of colonial trauma and the possibility of resistance on the side of the colonised. I will work towards identifying the discrepancies between indigenous and Western notions of trauma and identity, and study the challenges of postcolonial literatures. I will explore the concept of cultural hybridity as presented in the novels and study the impact of trauma on identity construction. In the process of this study, I intend to find out to what extent trauma influences and shapes identity. Moreover, I will reconsider the Western notions of trauma and identity and examine their integrity in the colonial discourse. With the help of the novels, I will study the differences between the antagonistic cultures and pursue the development of colonial trauma, which may shed a different light on the Western study of trauma. Moreover, I will explore the natives' means for dealing with the traumas brought about by the process of colonisation. My focus will be to explore how traumatised characters cope with living in a continuously distressing environment, the symptoms of their traumas and how these symptoms are expressed. Moreover, I will explore the conditions and means for resistance, and the process of the decolonisation of the mind. Furthermore, I will explore the authors' reasons and intentions for writing these novels.

In addition to it, in my analysis of psychic trauma in *Nervous Conditions*, I will draw a link to Franz Fanon's writings on psychoanalytic thought and his theory of decolonisation. Similarly to the novel, he analyses "the harm done to marginalised groups by continuous exposure to 'a galaxy of erosive stereotypes'."[1] With the aid of the novels I intend to study the analogies and differences between Dangarembga's and Highway's novels and Fanon's writings on gender, identity, violence and resistance to oppression.

1.2 Trauma Studies, Identity and Literature

This study will explore the fragmentation of identity as it is being transformed from the native identity to the colonial hybrid identity. The postcolonial novels demonstrate the process of colonial identity formation riven with cultural hybridity and ambiguity in a changing world. Among others, Franz Fanon's and Homi Bhabha's theories of cultural hybridity will be applied to the protagonists of the novels. The postcolonial novels illustrate cultural differences in identity construction. They depict the intermingling cultures of colonization which complicate the evolvement of an unambiguous stable identity. Moreover, the novelists explore the sociological component of identity formation. Westerners construct their identities as autonomous, independent selves, whereas indigenous peoples incorporate a sense of community into their identities. The Western basic framework "that sees the individual as distinct and distinguishable in the first place"[2] is problematic in the indigenous environment. In indigenous societies individuals are always part of a community and identify themselves with it. They cannot stand for themselves as solid independent individuals. In Africa, for example, "a person depends on other people to be a person."[3] In this context "community is essential to subjectivity [and] a person is incomplete unless he or

---

[1] Buelens, Gert, Steff Craps: "Introduction: Postcolonial Trauma Novels." *Studies in the Novel*, 40, 1/2 (2008), 3. Hereafter referred to as *Studies*.

[2] Murray, Jessica: A post-colonial and feminist reading of selected testimonies to trauma in post-liberation South Africa and Zimbabwe. *Journal of African Cultural Studies*, 21,1 (2009), 4. Here-after referred to as *Zimbabwe*.

[3] *Zimbabwe*, 4.

she maintains an active connection with the society or culture of which he or she is part."[4] This study will explore how these essential connections with native community are complicated and annihilated due to colonial intervention.

Moreover, the novels contribute to the discourse of trauma studies. Trauma studies as an area of cultural investigation came to prominence in the early-to-mid-1990s.[5] The relatively new discipline is committed to the ethical issues of trauma investigation. Cathy Caruth is "one of the leading figures in trauma studies," and argues that "a textualist approach [to trauma] can afford us unique access to history."[6] She purports that "the analysis of cultural artefacts that bear witness to traumatic histories, [can enable to] gain access to extreme events and experiences"[7] that constitute trauma. The scholars of trauma studies query the Western-biased approach to trauma and investigate the culture-bound deficiencies in trauma research. Caruth declares, "in its most general definition, trauma describes an overwhelming experience of sudden or catastrophic events in which the response to the event occurs in the often delayed, uncontrolled repetitive appearance of hallucinations or other intrusive phenomena."[8] The very definition of trauma sets an emphasis on "sudden, unexpected catastrophic events"[9] and, deriving from "the Greek word meaning wound,"[10] trauma has still predominantly a corporeal connotation in Western psychoanalysis. However, the colonial situation itself is inherently traumatising and has pathological consequences on the psyche of the colonised. Thus, the definition of trauma has been expanded by the analogy of the corporeal wound to "the wound of the mind."[11] The "feminist psychotherapist Laura S. Brown has argued" that colonial trauma is an "insidious trauma," by which "the traumatogenic effects of oppression that are not necessarily overtly violent or threatening to the bodily well-being at the given moment [...] do violence to the soul and spirit."[12] The novels *Nervous Conditions* and *Kiss of the Fur Queen* predominantly portray the expanded and revised notion of trauma, as trauma to the soul.

The recent developments in trauma studies call for a reconsideration of the applicability of Western trauma theories to colonial subjects by arguing that "current

---

[4] *Zimbabwe*, 4.
[5] Cp. *Studies*, 1.
[6] *Studies*, 1.
[7] *Studies*, 1.
[8] Caruth, Cathy: *Unclaimed Experience: Trauma, Narrative, and History*. Baltimore: John Hopkins University Press 1996, 11. Hereafter referred to as *Unclaimed*.
[9] *Studies*, 3.
[10] Luckhurst, Roger: *The Trauma Question*. London: Routledge 2008, 4. Hereafter referred to as *Question*.
[11] *Unclaimed*, 4.
[12] *Studies*, 3.

definitions of trauma have been constructed from the experiences of dominant groups in Western society."[13] The experiences of these dominant groups, however, do not include the chronic nature of trauma. Therefore, the chronic psychic suffering of the colonised has been commonly neglected in the Western study of trauma. The European or Western conception of trauma focuses traditionally on a single shocking and personally upsetting event which causes a psychopathology referred to as posttraumatic stress disorder (PTSD) in the victims. The traumatising effects of colonialism, however, have a different dimension. Colonialism encompasses a series of traumas for indigenous populations. Both novels illustrate the chronic nature of colonial trauma and its pathological effects on the colonised. Therefore, in my investigation of colonial trauma I will not focus on a single shocking event that causes trauma, but on a continuous accumulation and enhancement of traumatic stressors. I will analyse colonial trauma in terms of the symptoms of posttraumatic stress disorder and revise its applicability in the context of colonialism.

Another problem of the traditional study of trauma lies in its tendency to focus on individual psychology.[14] "Whereas earlier [trauma] research had focused on only single types of situations and victims," a more recent research of "the literature on traumatic stress" challenges this by mapping trauma as "a generalized and socialized phenomena."[15] Since colonisation constitutes a collective or cultural trauma, it is necessary to consider the wide scope of trauma. Following Sam Durrant, collective or cultural trauma disrupts "the 'consciousness' of the entire community [by] destroying the possibility of a common frame of reference and calling into question our sense of being-in-common."[16] Jessica Murray compares individual trauma to Durrant's notion of collective trauma. She writes, "as individual trauma overflows the individual victim's frame of reference, the trauma of colonialism 'disrupts the colonised culture's frame of reference'."[17] The indigenous societies' departure from the Western individual framework calls for a societal approach to colonial trauma. Thus the specificity of colonial trauma cannot be disclosed "unless the object of trauma research shifts from the individual to larger social entities, such as communities or nations."[18]

Furthermore, this study will explore the issues of healing, reconstruction and re-

---

[13] *Studies*, 3.
[14] Cp. *Studies*, 4.
[15] Vickroy, Laurie: *Trauma and Survival in Contemporary Fiction*. Charlottesville: University of Virginia Press 2002, 18. Hereafter referred to as *Survival*.
[16] *Zimbabwe*, 13.
[17] *Zimbabwe*, 13.
[18] *Studies*, 4.

sistance. The Western approaches to trauma therapy are insufficient for dealing with the traumatic experiences of subaltern groups. Due to the limited scope of knowledge about non-Western groups, trauma therapists often neglect the fact that other cultures have different ways of coping with trauma at their command. In the novels, I will explore alternative solutions for coming to terms with colonial trauma. Furthermore, I will investigate the protagonists' resistance to oppressive systems in terms of individual and national empowerment and trace their means for the reconstruction of their culture, self-knowledge and identity.

1.3 The Approach to Trauma in the Novels

Nervous Conditions is an exemplary novel of insidious trauma induced by colonial oppression and discrimination. The novel's traumatic conditions move away from the corporeal schema of trauma and expose trauma deriving from psychological damage. *Nervous Conditions* explores the traumatised condition of "the native" as a consequence of colonial intervention into the balance of traditional Shona culture in colonial Rhodesia (now Zimbabwe) of the late 1960s and early 1970s. Dangarembga's first-person narrator Tambudzai provides a sophisticated view into the coming-of-age consciousness of a teenage narrator struggling to cope and survive in a distorted colonial world. Tambudzai's complex identity provides the reader with an elaborate analysis of the sources underlying the nervous conditions of the colonised.

In *Nervous Conditions* the narrative focuses not only on colonial oppression but especially on sexual discrimination. The author subdivides the nervousness of the characters into gendered categories and provides an account of the extent of Westernization that pollutes and distorts the traditional gender roles. Tambu's anglicized cousin, Nyasha, is an influential character in the novel. She supports and guides Tambu's evolving identity. I will analyse the connections between Tambu's coming-of-age consciousness and Nyasha's appraisal of the colonial situation. The analysis of Nyasha's predicament in the novel, will concentrate on her deep cultural hybridity due to her early uprootedness. The patriarchal system will play a crucial role for my study of the main character's developing identity and her traumatic experiences. Belonging to the genre of *Bildungsroman,* the novel is a bright composition of the process of self-realization in relation to colonial analysis. I will query the nervous conditions in Dangarembga's novel with respect to its male and female characters and try to detect the triggers which enhance traumatic situations. I will study the psychopathological effects of the oppressed and analyse their means of coping with the situation. In terms of the indigenous and sexual empowerment, I will investigate the characters' ability to generate a resistance to oppression and colonisation.

Highway's partly autobiographical novel *Kiss of the Fur Queen* is an extreme exposition of trauma due to its incorporation of a twofold trauma—psychic and physic. The novel is set Manitoba, Canada, between 1951 and 1990, and tells a story of two young Cree brothers who are taken from their home and family and sent to a distant Catholic Residential School. In the boarding school the brothers are subjected to the whims of a sexually abusive principal of the school. It is a life narrative about diaspora, oppression, abuse, racism, violence and loss. The novel addresses the insidious consequences of colonial trauma, the author's way of coping with the unbearable situation, his identity problems and the issue of uprootedness on a very large scale. It is a life narrative about the different paths of two Indian brothers with a different outcome. Indigenous mythology and symbolism play an important role in the narrative. The author unveils the Cree world of spiritual mythology and legends, entwined with the Western cultural discourse. The novel is an exemplary narrative about cultural hybridity induced by Western influence and its consequences, and is a means for accommodating the novelist's personal trauma. I am interested in the study of the nature and effects of the trauma of the main characters. I will analyse the formation of the main characters' (post)colonial hybrid identities and explore their paths of self-realisation and reformation. Moreover, I will study the novel's political significance with respect to indigenous liberation and explore the significance of Indian mythology in Highway's novel. Thereby I will look at its meaning for his coping with trauma and the significance of the native set of symbols for approaching the brothers' traumatic experiences.

Since trauma studies need to "acknowledge traumatic experiences in non-Western settings,"[19] many scholars (have lately suggested theorizing colonization in terms of the infliction of a collective trauma and reconceptualising postcolonialism as a post-traumatic cultural formation). In order to (realize the self-declared ethical potential) of trauma studies, an examination of (postcolonial literary trauma representation) is necessary. This can achieve (a break with Eurocentrism). The analysis of postcolonial trauma (in relation to the dominant trauma discourse) can enable a modification of

---

[19]*Studies*, 1-3. All further references in the text are to this edition.

Western trauma theories (with a view to wider applicability). My intention is to detect alternative conceptions of trauma by analysing indigenous ways of coping, accommodating, communicating and combating the trauma of the past. The study will query the challenges the novels pose to the dominant discourse on trauma, identity and healing, and look for alternative solutions offered by the authors.

2. *Nervous Conditions*

2.1 Colonialism and Patriarchy

Tsitsi Dangarembga's (born 1959) first novel, *Nervous Conditions*, is the first novel published in English by a black Zimbabwean woman, and is the "winner of the African regional prize in the 1989 Commonwealth Writer's Prize competition."[20] The semi-autobiographical novel centres around two main female characters, Tambudzai (Tambu) and her anglicised cousin Nyasha, growing up in colonial Rhodesia. It is a first-person narrative told from Tambudzai's point of view. Dangarembga provides a sophisticated insight into the consciousness of a native coming-of-age character, Tambu, in her colonial environment, who has to endure colonialism and patriarchy. Tambu's highly self-reflexive analysis of her predicament as a young African woman growing up in a colonial world arises to a great extent from her accurate observation of her same-age cousin Nyasha, who suffers much more under the colonial situation in Rhodesia. Dangarembga's novel outlines the consequences of the British colonisation of Rhodesia, renamed Zimbabwe after its independence in 1980.[21] She illustrates the nuisances of "the colonial rule that extended from 1890 to 1979," during which "the white minority dominated and oppressed the native population and divested them of their land."[22]

The prologue of the novel—"*The condition of native is a nervous condition*" (v) —is taken "from Jean-Paul Sartre's preface to Franz Fanon's *The Wretched of the Earth*."[23] Although, following Dangarambga's words, "she had not read Fanon until the novel was competed,"[24] there are striking similarities between her book and Fanon's writings. Similarly to Fanon (1925-1961), Dangarembga had medical and psychological training before she started writing. In *The Wretched of the Earth* (1961) Fanon describes "the colonial world as a Manichaean world, in which the world of the native is the negation of the world of the settler."[25] Dangarembga goes beyond the limits of

---

[20] Thomas, Sue: "Killing the Hysteric in the Colonized's House: Tsitsi Dangarembga's 'Nervous Conditions'." *The Journal of Commonwealth Literature*, 27,1 (1992), 26. Hereafter referred to as *Hysteric*.

[21] Cp. Edwards, Justin D.: *Postcolonial Literature*. Basingstoke: Palgrave Macmillan 2008, 4. Hereafter referred to as *Literature*.

[22] *Literature*, 4.

[23] *Hysteric*, 26.

[24] Sugnet, Charles: "'Nervous Conditions': Dangarembga's Feminist Reinvention of Fanon." In: Obioma Nnaemeka (ed.): *The Politics of (M)Othering*. London: Routledge 1997, 35. Hereafter referred to as *Reinvention*.

[25] King, Bruce (ed.): *New National and Post-Colonial Literatures: An Introduction*. Oxford: Clarendon Press 1998, 122. Hereafter referred to as *National*.

"Fanons's canonical 'master narrative' of post-colonial psychiatric thought and literary criticism" and presents "patriarchal and colonial domination" from a woman's point of view. The author challenges Fanon by exploring "other psychological realities that [he] leaves unexamined— most specifically the role of gender in the colonial context."[26] In Dangarembga's critique of patriarchy she underlines how "the sexualities of native men and women are contained and mortified by colonialism and by Shona and Western patriarchy respectively."[27] With her novel, Dangarembga seems to imply that the condition of 'female' native has additional burdens.[28]

2.1.1 The Effects of Gendered Ideology

Nervous Conditions opens with the shocking breaking of a familial taboo in the form of Tambu's comment, "I was not sorry when my brother died. Nor am I apologising for my callousness, as you may define it, my lack of feeling" (1). The occasion of Tambu's brother's premature death is the first event that can be accounted for as traumatising due to colonialism, and it is the first event in the story that puts Tambu "in a position to write this account"(1). Her coldness towards her brother's death is a tragic sign of confusion and breakdown in social relations and cultural values under the pressure of colonisation. As Charles Sugnet underlines, Tambu's acknowledgement in the very first sentence of the novel that "I was not sorry when my brother died" is "perhaps the most important instance of an overt rupture"[29] of traditional familial bonds. In her "critical self-examination, [Tambu is] quite conscious about rejecting the guilt associated with 'unnatural' sisterhood, inhuman lack of feeling."[30] She says, "As he was our brother, he ought to be liked, which made disliking him all the more difficult" (11). She explains in the opening chapters of the novel how she came into the position to write this sentence. As Sugnet points out, "the whole novel is the story of how Tambudzai came to be capable of writing this sentence."[31] From Tambu's sophisticated analysis of her feelings towards her elder brother Nhamo, one can see the forces at work behind the colonial

---

[26] Scahatteman, Renee: *Fanon and Beyond: The 'Nervous Condition' of the Colonized Woman.* In: Kofi Anyidoho et al. (ed.): Beyond Survival: African Literatures & the Search for New Life. Trenton: Africa World Press 1998, 213. Hereafter referred to as *Beyond.*

[27] *Hysteric,* 27.

[28] Cp. Hawley, John C.: "Tsitsi Dangarembga's Ambiguous Adventure: Nervous Conditions and the Blandishments of Mission Education." In: Gerhard Stilz (ed.): *Missions of Interdependence. A Literary Directory.* Amsterdam: Rodopi 2002, 185. Hereafter referred to as *Adventure.*

[29] *Reinvention,* 39.

[30] Nair, Supriya: "Melancholic Women – The Intellectual Hysteric(s) in Nervous Conditions." *Research in African Literatures,* 26.2 (1995), 133.

[31] *Reinvention,* 39.

system. It is the intense clash of two distinct cultures and ideologies that causes dramatic imbalance and breaches familial bonds in traditional Shona families.

In Tambu's excuse for her lack of feelings for her brother, a crucial element comes to light, namely that of patriarchy. Colonial patriarchy worsens Tambu's condition as a colonial subject. Through her narration the reader can see the reasons for her "unnatural sisterhood" and for her repulsion towards Nhamo. Initially she likes him, which is normal for a sister. Later, however, her feelings drastically deteriorate as she is confronted with her brother's sexism. Tambu's first-hand experience of unfair inequality structures relying solely upon one's biological sex, uttered by her brother Nhamo, triggers her negative feelings towards him and initiates her nervous condition. His words, "I go to school. You go nowhere" (21) deeply shock her. Tambu recalls, "Nhamo was not interested in being fair. Maybe to other people, but certainly not to his sisters, his younger sisters for that matter"(12). The moment she learns that Nhamo blatantly advocates universal gender inequalities that preclude her from going to school, she states, "My concern for my brother died an unobtrusive death"(20). Nhamo fully approved the sexist mindset that boys shall have first access to education, and thus appropriated sexism into his repertoire of values.

Tambu depicts how effectively socialisation has worked on Nhamo and contributed to their alienation. Tambu recalls how he refused to carry his own bags and expected his sisters to carry them for him, and how he refused to help with housework. She complains about her "brother's laziness" and says, "I hated fetching my brother's luggage" (10). Worrying about his development, Tambu notes that "any of the tasks he used to do willingly before he went to the mission, became a bad joke" (7). Moreover, Nhamo tried to prevent his sister from going to school and thus oppressed her emancipation by overthrowing Tambu's attempt to grow maize to provide herself with school fees. This behaviour shows his affiliation with the patriarchal ideology. Disappointed in her brother, Tambu states that "our home was healthier when he was away" (10).

Since Nhamo's status as a boy and elder brother is a threat and an impediment to the education Tambu desires, his death is a coincidence which Tambu welcomes because it gives her the privilege of obtaining education in a "colonial system [which] makes education scarce."[32] Due to the fact that she has no elder siblings, she becomes next in line to receive colonial education at the mission school. The patriarchal system renders Nhamo's death not a tragedy to her but a salvation; she "could not have sur-

---

[32] *Reinvention*, 38.

vived on the homestead" (59). His death is celebrated as the occasion for her education at the mission school and an opportunity to become a full-fledged, educated person and escape the poverty of her native homestead. Tambu vindicates herself, "Thinking about it, feeling the injustice of it, this is how I came to dislike my brother […]"(12).

Moreover, Tambu observes her uncle Babamukuru's approval of sexism, apparent in his maltreatment of his wife and his daughter Nyasha. She comments on "Babamukuru condemning Nyasha to whoredom, making her a victim of her femaleness, just as I had felt victimised at home" (118). She states her indignation at sexual injustice that is fundamental to colonialism, "what I didn't like was the way all the conflicts came back to this question of femaleness. Femaleness as opposed and inferior to maleness" (118). Tambu identifies the malign nature of patriarchy, "The victimization, I saw, was universal. It didn't depend on poverty, on lack of education or on tradition" (118). Her realization of the scope of female oppression intensifies her traumatic realisation of gender inequalities. This realization about her uncle's sexism disillusions her image of him. Her previously immensely admired uncle, "who was as neatly divine as any human being could hope to be" (167), loses his reputation in her eyes. The disenchanted Tambu states, "Even heroes like Babamukuru did it" (118).

2.1.2 The Question of Masculinity

The novel investigates the relationship between native men and colonial authorities, and reveals another aspect of colonial patriarchy: the embodiment of Western cultural consensus on the level of political and socio-economic dominance. The colonial relationship between Europeans and natives was executed "in terms of the 'natural' ascendancy of men over women."[33] This notion of sexual dominance was transferred onto colonial masculinity and engendered an immense break in native masculinity by rendering it effeminate. The "racial effeminacy" of African men was analogous to the Western "dominance of men and masculinity over women and femininity."[34] The colonial congruence with "the existing Western sexual stereotypes and the philosophy of life which they represented"[35] deprived native men of their masculinity and created tension in the relationship between African men and women. African men in turn suppressed their women and thus participated in the double oppression and colonisation of the women nearest them. The novel suggests that "the existence of the colonized

---

[33] *Theory*, 100.
[34] *Theory*, 100.
[35] *Theory*, 100.

woman is invalidated by men of color in much the same way that the selfhood of all colonized people is annihilated by the Europeans."[36]

Moreover, the novel shows the sharp edges of colonial education offered to native African men. The patriarchal colonial rule sought to maintain its hegemony by electing African men who received colonial education. These men were catapulted to the colonial elite. This indirect rule facilitated the colonisation of the rest of the indigenous population through their 'traditional' leaders. Thus the colonial education of the African elite "served colonial economic and political needs."[37] Africans' "status as agents of colonial hegemony" offered "privilege, material reward, and apparent security."[38] Colonial education, however, has a double edge. It represents "literary and cultural temptations of Europe" and is a booster of "cultural transgression." [39] By transmitting Western values and belief systems, colonial education extinguishes the traditional values of the natives. It is an intricate tool to achieve the goal of colonial authorities, to colonise the mind of the natives.

The novel illustrates how colonial patriarchy works on African men as representatives of colonial hegemony. In the epigraph to the novel, Dangarembga omits the ensuing clause of Fanon's sentence, "The status of a 'native' is a nervous condition introduced and maintained by the settler among colonized people *with their consent.*"[40] The three most colonially implicated male characters of the novel, Babamukuru (Jeremiah's elder brother), Nhamo and Chido (Babamukuru's son), "give a sort of coerced consent to their status as agent[s] of colonial hegemony."[41] The colonial system offers Babamukuru a privileged position. He was able to receive colonial university education in South Africa and attain his Master's degree in England. In return for his academic career and prosperity, which enables his position as the provider for his extended family, he has to fulfil many obligations. He works for the colonial system and is the headmaster of the mission school which Tambu wishes to attend. He represents the system's indirect ruler who works as a transformer between the colonial authority and the marginalised natives, and whose law "becomes the law of the white men."[42] Therefore, Babamukuru impersonates a traditional leader. Sugnet underlines, "with all

---

[36] *Beyond*, 213.
[37] Ania Loomba: *Colonialism, Postcolonialism*. London: Routledge 2002, 139. Hereafter referred to as *Colonialism*.
[38] *Reinvention*, 38.
[39] Gandhi, Leela: *Postcolonial Theory, a Critical Introduction*. Edinburgh: Edinburgh University Press 1998, 13. Hereafter referred to as *Theory*.
[40] *Reinvention*, 38.
[41] *Reinvention*, 38.
[42] *Colonialism*, 145.

his advanced degrees and Christian ways, Babamukuru [is an] impressive kind of 'native,' created by the British colonial system to serve its purposes."[43]

Dangarembga reveals Babamukuru's plight in the novel, where he is torn apart by his desperate attempt to maintain a traditional Shona family and simultaneously apply to them Western Christian values. When he plays "the part of the 'good kaffir' of the colonizer's imagination,"[44] he suffers from 'bad nerves' and is only able to alleviate his nervousness when he is far away from the centre of colonial authority, on the country-side. In a rare moment in the novel, he remembers his boyhood and starts to hum an old song and is spontaneously happy: "Unaccountably, unusually, Babamukuru was happy. Free of tensions and in the best of spirits, he looked younger and more lovable than he ever did at the mission" (124–25).[45] Sugnet emphasises, "the farther he gets from his English-made job and personality, the farther he gets from his nervous condition."[46] When Babamukuru is in the centre of his colonial responsibility he is ill-tempered. One evening, when he returns to his house, he is moody and avoids greeting his family; "Babamukuru grunted briefly by way of reply, in a way that told you at once that he had weightier matters on his mind than the goodness of the evening" (81). Tambu utters her disappointment in her uncle's behaviour after she moves to his house. She deplores that his behaviour has changed and he became more aloof than he used to be before he left for England: "I had thought it would be like the good old days [...] with Babamukuru throwing us up in the air and giving us sweets" (104). She continues: "We hardly ever laughed [...] we did not talk much when he was around either" (104). His wife, Mai-guru, explains, "His nerves were bad because he was so busy" (104). The deterioration of Babamukuru's behaviour signals his nervous condition which is a far-reaching consequence of his colonial education.

Tambu's father, Jeremiah, is a 'historical artefact' as well, constructed and main-tained by the colonial system. His traditional patriarchal dependency on his elder brother, Babamukuru, is colonially induced. Colonial authorities deprived him of his ancestral lands, thus making him incapable of providing for his family and fully dependent on his brother's financial support. Sugnet argues that Jeremiah "becomes the stereotype of the shiftless 'native', spending his children's school fees on beer and letting his homestead run down."[47] As a result, he "embodies a parodic debasement of

---

[43] *Reinvention*, 36.
[44] *Hysteric*, 26.
[45] Cp. *Reinvention*, 37.
[46] *Reinvention*, 37.
[47] *Reinvention*, 36.

13

'traditional' values."[48] Jeremiah suffers from the loss of his patriarchal authority as father of his children. When Tambu's teacher, Mr Matimba, helps her with selling her mealies and keeps her money in safety for her school fees, Jeremiah complains, "Does he think he is your father? [...] He thinks that because he has chewed more letters than I have, he can take over my children. And you, you think he is better than me" (24). He also mistreats his wife, Mainini. In the novel, Dangarembga connects male suffering under the colonial system with the men's impulse to bully the women in their families.[49]

2.1.3 The Burden of Femininity

The colonial system renders Tambu and other native women doubly oppressed. In the Rhodesian colonial context female subordination is maintained by the cultural consensus that regards women as second-class citizens. The author reveals the system of double oppression: the British colonial authority oppresses the male indigenous population and indigenous men themselves oppress their women. Tambu elucidates, "the needs and sensibilities of the women in my family were not considered a priority, or even legitimate" (12). Even Tambu's father, Jeremiah, sides with the oppressive system and operates as an antagonist to Tambu's educational prospect. His comment, "Can you cook books and feed them to your husband?" (15), shows his native patriarchy entwined with solidarity for the oppressive colonial system. Ketu H. Katrak elucidates that "in general, female education, governed by Victorian ideology and Christian missionary zeal, was aimed at producing women as good wives and mothers."[50] In this context the burden of femininity poses a direct threat to Tambu's highly desired education.

Furthermore, Dangarembga illustrates Nyasha's desperate attempt to free herself from the patriarchal oppression. Her struggle for emancipation within Rhodesia is a precarious matter, because her sexuality is a contested term. Nyasha's uprootedness makes it (increasingly difficult for her to belong within the constraints of traditional patriarchal norms embodied in and enforced by her father Babamukuru). Nyasha cannot fulfil the traditional expectations of female obedience and silence, and her father's (attempts to have a 'traditional' daughter, obedient to his will, backfire in the terrible dramas around food). Her European influenced view of women is at odds with the African concept of female subordination, and her struggle to free herself from the

---

[48] *Reinvention*, 36.
[49] Cp. *Reinvention*, 36.
[50] *National*, 233. All further references in the text are to this edition.

traditional expectations of her father ends tragically in her ailment anorexia nervosa or bulimia when she (attempts to take control over her life). Additionally, the intersection of education provided by the mission with the patriarchal elements of the Shona culture increases her plight. Though Nyasha has gained a critical apparatus in England with which help she is able to analyse critically the whole colonial situation, she is incapable of leading a traditional Shona life because "she has also picked up English social expectations that disrupt her acceptance of patriarchal social norms."[51] Her hybrid identity poses her between the antagonistic cultures and renders her an outsider within her native Shona community.

Dangarembga delineates how Babamukuru oppresses his well-educated wife, Maiguru, who holds a Master's degree in Philosophy from London and has her own job. Maiguru struggles to cope with the oppressive social situation. She has to give away her entire salary for the sustenance of Babamukuru's relatives and is unable "to stand up to her husband or protect her daughter."[52] Tambu remarks, "[…] it was a great shame that Maiguru had been deprived of the opportunity to make the most of herself, even if she had accepted that deprivation" (103). Maiguru's inability to act alone under oppressive circumstances and keep her salary to herself causes her daughter Nyasha to lose respect of her. Maiguru has to fulfil the traditional expectations of an obedient and good wife is spite of her European education. She is at pains to comply with the Shona tradition and fulfil the obligations of a working wife and mother. Caught in her powerless situation, she desperately laments, "I am not happy. I am not happy any more in this house" (175). As the only Western-educated woman of her native community she is not accepted among other married women. Her desperate situation shows how "English education […] renders educated women into outsiders in their own communities."[53]

The horizontal oppression unleashes the nervous conditions of all the characters in the novel. As such, the chain reaction of patriarchal oppression imposes a threat to the mental and physical health of the colonised. Maiguru and Mainini "both give numerous hints of the repressed rage they harbour over their assigned roles through their attempt to hide these feelings."[54] The oppressed women of the novel are frequently character-ised by silence. In many instances in the novel, female characters refrain from uttering their opinions. They reluctantly comply with the traditional silence of women unless

[51] *Adventure*, 186.
[52] *Reinvention*, 39.
[53] *National*, 233.
[54] *Beyond*, 214.

asked. Especially for the partly Western educated Maiguru, the situation is difficult to endure. Her excessive submissiveness unnerves her extremely. Mainini's attitude of indifference is her reaction to oppression. Tambu also suffers under the oppressive situation and often has a need to say what she thinks. Justin D. Edwards outlines Pauline Ada Uwakweh's argumentation that "silence is used as a patriarchal weapon of control" for the reason that "voicing is self-defining, liberational, and cathartic."[55] When the powerful Babamukuru "tries to silence all the women in the family,"[56] his daughter, Nyasha, accurately designates her father "a historical artefact" (162). The concept of a 'historical artefact' stems from Franz Fanon[57] and Dangarembga extends his concept to native women. Her novel demonstrates that not only native men, but also native women are not natural but 'historical artefacts' constructed by the oppressive colonial system.[58] Dangerambga describes "the struggles of the young Tambu against the immediate manifestations of patriarchy in her life."[59] Mainini's predicament shows her powerless-ness and hopelessness, and even Maiguru is denied agency, control and even identity. Concerning all these characters, the novel shows how female "self and sexuality are constructed and controlled by indigenous patriarchy and British colonial practices,"[60] and "how patriarchy and colonisation collude to worsen women's predicament."[61]

2.2 Identity and Hybridity

Nervous Conditions introduces two main characters with complex identities— Tambudzai and Nyasha. Dangarembga's coming-of-age novel explores colonial identities in a society in transition. The main protagonist, Tambu, provides a self-reflective and lucid analysis of her highly complex identity. Tambu grows up on an impoverished farm with her family. Nyasha spends five of her formative years with her parents in England. When Tambu's brother dies, she is thirteen. She moves to her uncle's house, where she becomes close to his daughter Nyasha. Nyasha's hybridity is the result of the years she spent in England. The novel explores the formation of colonial identity and offers sophisticated answers to questions of colonial and post-colonial identity. In the novel, Tambu takes readers on the journey of "constant recon-

---

[55] *Literature*, 103.
[56] *Reinvention*, 33.
[57] Cp. *Reinvention*, 38.
[58] Cp. *Reinvention*, 38.
[59] *Reinvention*, 34.
[60] *National*, 232.
[61] *National*, 232.

struction and reinvention of the self."[62] Her cousin Nyasha is her companion and sometimes guides her on that journey.

The novel expands the standard Western identity model which focuses on identity as being (a stable, self-contained agent). Instead, it focuses on the analysis of identity as becoming (a process of constructing, negotiating and, not least, maintaining).[63] Dangarembga's delineation of the process of colonial identity construction in the novel complies with Stuart Hall's appeal to reconsider the issue of identity and to depart from the Western concept of stable identity. Hall proposes "to appropriate it to designate identity as a constructed process rather than a given essence."[64] He points out, "the black subject and black experience are [also] constructed historically, culturally, politically."[65]

The novel shows how the African notion of identity gets fragmented and polluted by the appropriation of Western modes of individual autonomy. The novel illustrates "how cultural hybridity causes the individual to be pulled in multiple directions, adopting identities which may differ from each other."[66] Tambu's and Nyasha's hybrid identities exemplify the "modes of experiencing and constructing difference."[67] Eslamieh explains the genesis of a colonial/postcolonial hybrid: "The identity of both the colonizer and the colonized within a postcolonial society evolves into a hybrid identity, since colonisation creates spaces that are corporal positions of multiplicity."[68] With the aid of Dangarembga's novel, we can observe and explore the steps of colonial identity formation, a process which involves fragmentation, ambiguity, splitting, mimicry and re-creation of the colonised self.

---

[62] Pristed, Helene: "The Concept of Identity." In: Wojciech H. Kalaga et al. (ed.): *Multicultural Dilemmas: Identity, Difference, Otherness.* Frankfurt am Main: Lang 2008, 35.

[63] Cp. Kunow, Rüdiger, Wilfred Raussert (ed.): *Cultural Memory and Multiple Identities.* Berlin: Lit 2008, 7.Hereafter referred to as *Memory.*

[64] Loomba, Ania: *Colonialism, Postcolonialism.* London: Routledge 1998, 176. Hereafter referred to as *Postcolonialism.*

[65] *Postcolonialism*, 176.

[66] Eslamieh, Salumeh: "Tsitsi Dangarembga's 'Nervous Conditions': Coming of Age and Adolescence as Representative of Multinational Hybridity." *Moveable Type: Childhood and Adolescence*, 1.1 (2005). <http://www.ucl.ac.uk/english/graduate/issue/1_1/salumeh.htm> (04.11.2011). Hereafter referred to as *Adolescence.*

[67] *Memory*, 7.

[68] *Adolescence.*

2.2.1 The Distortion of Identity

Dangarembga demonstrates how colonialism disrupts and distorts mother-child relationships and hinders the female protagonists' healthy identification with the mother. The mother's role is especially important in nurturing and socialising her children. Laurie Vickroy emphasises Jessica Benjamin's point that "the mother must have her own independent identity to be able to give the child the recognition it wants and guide its healthy development."[69] The oppressive system deprives mothers of their own identities and renders them (deeply conflicted between the social demands of motherhood, their own needs, and their children's well-being). Dangarembga successfully presents how mothers are (continually denied their point of view or status as subjects in oppressive systems [and] how their limited scope of action becomes destructive of themselves and their children). She delineates how (a mother's role is compromised when mechanisms of oppressive control [...] limit her options and rights). Tambu illustrates her mother's subjugation: "for most of her life my mother's mind, belonging first to her father and then to her husband, had not been hers to make up" (155).

The colonial interference in the lives of the natives impedes Tambu's identification with her parents. She disapproves of her parents as role models and instead admires her partly English educated uncle, Babamukuru, and his wife, Maiguru. Tambu states: "I decided it was better to be like Maiguru, who was not poor and had not been crushed by the weight of womanhood" (16). She disapproves of her parents' way of life and their attitudes. Tambu regards her mother's thinking in binary oppositions of good versus evil, indigenousness versus Englishness, as inadequate and distances herself from it. She comprehends that there must be paths other than remaining completely uncontaminated by Englishness, or the opposite direction, becoming completely Westernised. She condemns her mother's "history of compromise, and her tendency toward passivity and paralysis,"[70] and disapproves of her appeal "to learn to carry [her] burdens" of "poverty [and] blackness" "with strength" (16). As for her father, Jeremiah, she cannot approve of his laziness and his spending of the money for school fees on beer. Jeremiah lets the homestead run down so much that she has to intervene and mend it herself. She abhors his patriarchal thinking and says: "I discovered to my unhappy relief that my father was not sensible" (16). Thus the novel shows how the colonially

---

[69] Vickroy, Laurie: *Trauma and Survival in Contemporary Fiction.* Charlottesville: University of Virginia Press 2002, 51. Hereafter referred to as *Survival.* All further references in the text are to this edition.

[70] *Reinvention*, 40.

imposed hindrance of a neat identification with the mother contributes to the fragmentation of Tambu's identity.

Tambu's estrangement from her parents amplifies when she leaves for the mission. Her father becomes "insignificant" and her mother "superfluous, an obstacle in the path of [her] departure" (58). Instead she looks up to her educated uncle and aunt, until she learns that they, too, are not perfect. Bit by bit she spots their flaws and becomes disappointed and frustrated. When she figures out that her uncle is not an exception when it comes to patriarchy, and Maiguru knowingly succumbs to the predicament of femininity, even though she is educated, Tambu's faith in her role models gets shaken and she has to reorientate herself. Since it is important for healthy identity formation for one to have role models to identify with, the inconsistency of her role models poses additional burdens to Tambu's evolving identity.

Moreover, Tambu experiences a break with the traditional concept of identity which assumes community and culture as key resources for identity formation. Instead she strives for autonomy and independence. She develops an individualistic thinking characteristic of the West. The first instance of the rupture of familial bonds and communal sense is evident in Tambu's inauguration of the novel. Her lack of condolence for her brother's premature death and her intense desire for colonial education are indicative of the Western influence. Tambu's wish for colonial education can be measured as her embrace of Western individual success. When Nhamo dies Tambu explains that his loss is not her loss: "I was not sorry that he had died, but I was sorry for him because, according to his standards, his life had been thoroughly worth living" (56). This comment accentuates the break of traditional familial bonds and shows Tambu's aspiration for Western individual success. Moreover, Tambu's acceptance of Nhamo's "death as the price of her own freedom"[71] presents colonialism as a disease that infects and destroys indigenous familial relations.

Her brother Nhamo's changed identity shows how colonial influence disrupts traditional values. Dangarembga depicts the chain of education, acculturation, alienation and disavowal that leads to his changed identity before his death of mumps. When he moves to the mission, he gradually assumes his new Westernised identity. Tambu recalls: "when Nhamo came home at the end of his first year with Babamukuru, you could see he too was no longer the same person. The change in his appearance was dramatic" (52). Nhamo starts disliking the homestead and disapproves of the whole

---

[71] *Reinvention*, 39.

situation there. He only reluctantly goes home, and stops speaking his native Shona. Instead he starts speaking English and appropriates Western behavioural manners. He removes himself physically and mentally from the homestead and his family there, and is intent on taking on his new identity because it offers him privilege and security, which he cannot expect on the homestead. Tambu notes his alienation: "my brother had become a stranger to me" (56). Nhamo is ashamed of the poverty of the homestead and even of his parents: "'[...] I shall no longer be Jeremiah's son,' he shouted, speaking [his] father's name in such derogatory tones" (48). Renee Schatteman argues that Nhamo represents most evidently "the desperate imitation of whiteness" as he abandons his father's name.[72] As for his mother, Tambu recollects, "he did not speak to her very often any more" (53). His behaviour shows the break of familial bonds and reveals that Nhamo denies his "own cultural identity for a comfortable place in the social pecking order."[73]

Dangarembga depicts the compromised identity of her main character. Tambu suffers from the inequalities of the oppressive patriarchal system, which establish in her a sense of her own superfluity. Before Nhamo's death her imminent exclusion from education, preserved for boys only, triggers an identity crisis in Tambu. She reasons, "Exclusion whispered that my existence was not necessary [...] that the process had gone wrong and produced me instead of another Nhamo, another Chido, another Babamukuru-to-be. I often felt superfluous in those days" (40). Tambu's self-perception is recomposed when she leaves her home and parents behind and grasps enthusiastically the opportunity that would lead her to her "destination" (58). She experiences a drastic break in her personality. Tambu equates her formal welcome at her new place with a formal disinterment of her mind and body from the village.[74] On the mission, she depicts the advent of her new identity, "Thus began the period of my reincarnation" (94). Dangarembga explicitly outlines Tambu's alternating identities when she moves. Tambu analyses, "This was the person I was leaving behind. At Babamukuru's I expected to find another self, a clean, well-groomed, genteel self" (58). These adjectives symbolise the Western appearance she strives to assume at Babamukuru's. Tambu adds that "this new me" "could not have been bred, could not have survived, on the home-stead" (59). Tambu is intent on becoming "a young woman of the world" (94) and willingly sheds her old traditional self.

---

[72] *Beyond*, 210.
[73] Survival, 43.
[74] Cp. Dangarembga, Tsitsi: *Nervous Conditions*. Banbury: Ayebia Clarke Publishing Ltd. 2004, 87.

However, Tambu is very soon disillusioned with her life at Babamukuru's house. When Tambu sees her uncle's big white house and the wealth that exceeds what she had imagined, she realises that there is a deep breach between her and Babamukuru. She states, "A deep valley cracked open. There was no bridge; at the bottom, spiked crags as sharp as spears. I felt separated forever from my uncle" (64). This realisation "became very depressing and confusing" (65). Tambu states that the dust in the house which was responsible for her hay fever was "restoring your sense of proportion by reminding you that this was not heaven" (71). Moreover, Tambu depicts her initial ambiguous feelings towards her anglicised cousin Nyasha on the mission. The ambiguity results from Nyasha's acculturation and estrangement due to her Western socialisation. Tambu delineates her split consciousness: "I was intrigued and fascinated with one part of my mind, the adventurous, exploitative part. But ... most of me sought order. ... These parts disapproved of Nyasha very strongly and were very wary of her" (76). This shows her shifting selves caught in the ambiguity of the colonial condition.

Tambu analyses how her embrace of the Western modes of life makes her identity ambiguous and elusive. Tambu describes the transformation that follows her relocation to the mission as a distressing experience and self-alienation. She recounts how her ambiguity irritated her mother, "made my mother wonder whether I was quite myself, or whether I was carrying some other presence in me" (94). She mourns a rather woeful development in her new place. She is worried about her new self on the mission which, being caught in "a bed of confusion," has become "unnatural" (167). Furthermore, she says that her "vagueness and reverence for [her] uncle" has "sapped the energy" that she had used "in childhood [...] to define [her] own position" (167). Tambu assesses the loss of her ability to assert herself as a very unsatisfactory feature of her new identity. She states, "I do not know how I came to be like that. ... I had grown very tentative" (112). She stresses the trouble of her new identity, "My going to the mission was such a drastic change that it unnerved me" (112).

The turning point for Tambu's negotiation of identity arises at the prospect of her parents' church wedding, insisted on by her uncle Babamukuru. A dramatic challenge strains her realization of self. Dangarembga portrays how colonial education engenders ambiguity and splits the identity of the colonised by teaching them racist facts that "black would remain definitely sombre and white permanently clear" (167). Tambu's identity is compromised through her education, which conveys Christian values "such as that 'sin is black,' and [she] does accept them."[75] The performance of a Christian ritual in a Rhodesian setting induces a stark clash of belief systems which queries Tambu's very existence. The incompatibility of Christian and indigenous belief systems induces a vehement identity crisis in teen Tambu. She declares that the wedding "placed doubt on [her] legitimate existence in this world" (165). Her split identity is explicitly described in the trains of thought regarding her parents' wedding. She says that "the advantages and disadvantages of white lace and vows at this late stage battled about in [her] head" (166) and "made a mockery of the people [she] belonged to" (165). Tambu realizes that "this wedding was a farce" (167). Therefore, she "could not approve of the wedding" "with half of [her] mind, but in the other half the black square of sin reap-peared and grew to an alarming size" (165). With this utterance she shows her splitting due to the incorporation of Christian values into her belief system. Moreover, her assigned role as a bridesmaid in her parents' wedding makes her anxious. She says, "My role in the comedy had been confirmed and rehearsed, but I still did not want to take part" (166).

2.2.2 Mimicry and Early Childhood

Nyasha's identity undergoes the most radical transformation of all the characters in the novel. Her early relocation to the colonial metropolis when she is only five years old entails an irreversible break with her African identity. The five years she spends in England with her parents turn her into a cultural hybrid. During her formative years in England she is exposed to English culture and language, and this early exposure brings about the loss of her African identity since she is too young to remember her early life before her time in England. Upon her return to Rhodesia she is another person. Tambu complains about the change in her appearance, "I missed the bold, ebullient companion I had had who had gone to England but not returned from there" (52). Her looks and behaviour have changed by assuming English ways.

Nyasha's mimicry of the English exemplifies Homi Bhabha's concept of mimicry. Nyasha represents the ambivalent 'mimic man'. She is caught in a situation of hate and desire for the colonial metropolis. On the one hand she is attracted to Europe, but on the other hand she despises it. Dimple Godiwala argues that according to Bhabha, the colonised subject "mimics because he or she has internalised the notion that their

---

[75] *Reinvention*, 43.

cultural values are inferior to that of the colonials."[76] Due to Nyasha's early relocation, her mimicry of English culture is produced "quite unconsciously as she internalizes and repeats implicitly [its] values."[77] Godiwala delineates that for Bhabha, "the anglicization of a colonial subject makes the subject familiar and yet, [...] emphasises the difference from the English subject which is a process that mocks the authority of the latter."[78] Thus, Leela Gandhi emphasises that Nyasha's anglicisation unleashes "the construction of a politically conscious, unified revolutionary Self, standing in unmitigated opposition to the oppressor."[79]

Nyasha's deep cultural hybridity is developed and performed unconsciously due to her early exposure to English socialisation. Unlike Tambu, she cannot change her behavioural pattern and assume her indigenous identity because her deeply hybridised nature is beyond her control. Nyasha complains, "They think we do it on purpose...I can't help having been there and grown into the me that has been there" (79). She complains that her parents are now "stuck with hybrids for children," which "they don't like" and which "offends them" (79). Tambu mourns the dramatic change in her cousins, "Now they had turned into strangers. I stopped being offended and was sad instead" (43). Nyasha's alienation and acculturation make her ignorant of traditional rites and thus remove her further from her aspiration to belong. She and her brother Chido can barely speak and understand Shona any more. She has barely any friends at school and her cultural hybridity makes it increasingly difficult for her to belong in Rhodesia.

Nyasha's early English socialisation poses the main difference between Tambu's and Nyasha's developing identities. Nyasha is disconnected from the Shona culture and her people because she cannot retrieve the memories of her early childhood. Tambu, however, can hold to her "rootedness in childhood, the Zimbabwean landscape, and her own female body," evident in "much of the early narrative [which] captures the felt immediacy of the presocialized child."[80] These memories give Tambu strength and points of orientation as she ascends the social ladder and absorbs Christian messages that collude with her childhood memories. In her childhood memories "she seems to

---

[76] Godiwala, Dimple: "Response to Homi Bhabha's Theory of 'Mimicry'." In: Joel Kuortti et al.: *Reconstructing Hybridity: Postcolonial Studies in Transition.* Amsterdam: Rodopi 2007, 61.Hereafter referred to as *Response.*
[77] *Response,* 61.
[78] *Response,* 60.
[79] *Theory,* 11.
[80] *Reinvention,* 40.

own her own body"[81] and is yet uncontaminated by gender differences which she later condemns. She recalls the bliss and jauntiness of the bathing areas before they were overrun by the colonial commercial system. She says, "when I was feeling brave, which was before my breasts grew too large, I would […] run down the river, slip off my frock […] and swim blissfully for as long as I dared in the old deep places" (4). As Sugnet notes, her frock "marks both gender difference and British colonialism."[82] Thus Sugnet argues that Tambu's rootedness in the "old deep places" of the river Nyamarira, where she could play as she pleased, functions as a touchstone of her identity.

The difference between Tambu's and Nyasha's early childhood makes Nyasha's identity more complex. The politically sophisticated Nyasha, who "had taken seriously the lessons about oppression and discrimination that she had learnt first-hand in England" (64) "does not have such 'old deep places' to orient herself."[83] Heather Zwicker argues that "Nyasha's relationship to Shona culture has been formalized into an almost anthropological interest in traditional crafts like basket-making."[84] Even though she is outspoken in her critique of colonialism, "she has no connections to protect her when she does speaks out," for "she has no other culture with which to connect."[85] This missing connection complicates Nyasha's identity formation since, unlike Tambu, she has no bedrock in which to build her identity.

2.2.3 The Ambiguity of White Masks

The novelist discloses the harm done to the colonised identity and supports many of Fanon's and Bhabha's theories about the insidious consequences of the colonial enterprise. The novel unveils striking similarities with Frantz Fanon's *Black Skin, White Masks* (1952) and *The Wretched of the Earth*. Fanon's psychoanalytical work condemns colonialism for the disruptive forces it releases on the side of the colonised. He claims that colonialism "dislocated and distorted the colonised's psyche" and "eroded his very being, his very subjectivity."[86] He further suggests that "the colonial experience

---

[81] *Reinvention*, 40.
[82] *Reinvention*, 41.
[83] *Reinvention*, 41.
[84] Zwicker, Heather: "The Nervous Collusions of Nation and Gender: Tsitsi Dangarembga's Challenge to Fanon." In: Treiber Jeanette et al. (ed.): *Negotiating the Postcolonial: Emerging Perspectives on Tsitsi Dangarembga*. Trenton: Africa World Press 2002, 19. Hereafter referred to as *Collusions*.
[85] Sizemore, Christine W.: "Negotiating Between Ideologies: The Search for Identity in Tsitsi Dangarembga's 'Nervous Conditions' and Margret Atwood's 'Cat's Eye'." *Women's Studies Quarterly*, 25.3/4 (1997), 73. Hereafter referred to as *Negotiating*.
[86] *Colonialism*, 142-43.

annihilates the colonised's sense of self."[87] *Nervous Conditions* mirrors his position with regard to colonialism. Fanon describes the colonial condition "as psychopathological, a disease that distorts human relations and renders everyone within it 'sick'."[88] The novel demonstrates, quite in Fanon's sense, how the process of colonisation distorts human relationships and erodes the very subjectivity of the colonised. Tambu's mother Mainini makes consistent references to 'Englishness', which she relates to colonialism. She identifies Englishness as a deadly social disease, with an ability to destroy one's identity and split families apart. It is depicted as a symbolic sickness that poses danger to the life of colonial society, brought about by the process of colonialism. She blames Englishness for the alienation of her children. Mainini warns Tambu, "Tell me, my daughter, what will I, your mother say to you when you come home a stranger full of white ways and ideas? It will be English, English, all the time" (187). When she speaks of the anglicised siblings Nyasha and Chido, she blames 'Englishness' for their plight: "'It's Englishness'... 'It'll kill them all if they are not careful'" (207).

Nyasha's deep cultural hybridity shows the serious consequences of Englishness as symptomatic of the infection of Western influence. In *Black Skin, White Masks* Fanon analyses "the harm done to marginalised groups by continuous exposure to 'a galaxy of erosive stereotypes' (129), which causes them to develop feelings of inferiority, inadequacy, and self-hatred."[89] Similarly, in the novel, Nyasha's exposure to Western concepts of beauty provokes in her feelings of inadequacy and thus the urge to adjust. Nyasha has internalised the European ideal of female beauty and tries to adjust to it by reducing her food intake. She prefers angles to curves and disapproves of Tambu's traditional female physique, "Pity about the backside... It is rather large" (92). In a possible transference of *Black Skin, White Masks* onto Nyasha's character, she becomes the black person "adopting white masks."[90] The white mask causes a disturbing experience in a black subject because there is always a gap between the black skin and white mask. This gap is marked by the impossibility to transcend it. By putting on a white mask the black subject tries to "make the fact of his blackness vanish," but never succeeds. This disturbs his or her psyche and shatters his or her very being. Nyasha's depiction in the novel supports Fanon's argument that "the colonial subject cannot escape the blackness of the skin and is 'forever in combat with his own image'."[91]

---

[87] *Colonialism*, 143.
[88] *Colonialism*, 143.
[89] *Studies*, 3.
[90] *Colonialism*, 145.
[91] *Beyond*, 209.

Schatteman argues that Nyasha "is an extreme embodiment of the white-masked black with her desire for slimness, her definite British accent and her western concepts of feminism."[92] Nevertheless, her white mask cannot make the fact of her black skin vanish and thus, tragically, advances her into nothingness. The tension between performance and appearance prompts Nyasha's self-destructive behaviour and leads her into anorexia. This inescapable situation traumatises Nyasha's psyche, as for Fanon "psychic trauma results when the colonised subject realises that he can never attain the whiteness he has been taught to desire, or shed the blackness he has learnt to devalue."[93] This situation of imitation "reflects the miserable schizophrenia of the colonized identity."[94] This tension suggests, as Bhabha argues, that "colonial identities are always a matter of flux and agony."[95]

Bhabha amplifies Fanon's image of black skin/white masks by arguing that there is not 'a neat division' but (a doubling, dissembling image of being in at least two places at once). This disturbing image of ambiguity displaces the colonial subject. Following Bhabha, (the disturbing distance in between constitutes the figure of colonial otherness—the White man's artifice inscribed on the Black man's body). He maintains, (it is in relation to this impossible object that emerges the liminal problem of colonial identity and its vicissitudes). The colonial situation turns Nyasha into an outsider, neither English nor African. She suffers immensely from her predicament and complains about the distortion of her self, "I was comfortable in England but now I'm a whore with dirty habits" (119). Nyasha's English is much better than that of the rest of her peers. It sounds more natural and renders her an outsider. Nyasha learns painfully that "to speak in the desired way [means], from now on, [also] to speak against oneself."[96] She suffers from exclusion from her classmates: "As it turned out, it was not Nyasha's accent they disliked, but Nyasha herself. 'She thinks, she is white,' they used to sneer, and that was a bad curse" (95). Later Nyasha describes her distressing situation in a letter to Tambu:

---

[92] Scahatteman, *Fanon and Beyond*, p. 211
[93] *Postcolonialism*, 176.
[94] *Colonialism*, 145.
[95] *Postcolonialism*, 176. All further references in the text are to this edition.
[96] *Theory*, 13.

They do not like my language, my English, because it is authentic and my Shona, because it is not! They think that I am a snob, that I think I am superior to them because I do not feel that I am inferior to men. [...] I very much would like to belong, [...] but I find I do not. (200)

Nyasha's ambiguity demonstrates that she "clearly occupies 'the space of splitting' that Bhabha refers to."[97] On the one hand, she is an extreme embodiment of Fanon's (white-masked black [but] on the other hand, she defends her blackness by preferring a black mission school to the nun's institution). She also prefers the traditional cleansing ceremony to the Christian wedding for Tambu's parents. As Schatteman points out, (Nyasha painfully recognises the schism in herself when she states, "I'm not one of them but I'm not one of you" (205)). Nyasha is the exemplary agonising character that validates Fanon's argument that "colonialism was the cause which engendered psychic differences along racial lines and annihilated the black subject into nothingness."[98]

Dangarembga's novel reveals "the enduring struggles that have formed the identities of her people and what it means to be African"[99] in a multicultural society. Nyasha's and Tambu's identities are always in a process of becoming, never achieving a fixed stable position. As Sugnet elucidates, in the colonial context of Rhodesia, Nyasha and Tambu cannot find a simple identity as 'African' or 'woman', "because both are contested terms undergoing continuous revision," and "for both Tambu and Nyasha, identity will be a shifting third term."[100] The cultural clash challenges their identities, and places them in a constant negotiation and reformation of the self. Tambu's self-analysis is at the same time her realisation of that fact. The novel delineates how she negotiates between her multiple identities in search for the appropriate one. On her identity quest, she undergoes a journey of analysis, assessment and compromise as she seeks her true self in the constantly traumatising situation. Tambu's coming of age, and her consistent refrains to "this new me" in the novel, function "as a theory of rebirth for oneself within evolving society."[101] Salumeh Eslamieh points out, (Tambu serves as a pioneer of hybrid autonomy because she is able to transcend the corporal position of the nervous condition). He argues, (as Tambu transitions from the homestead, mission, and convent, she enters the metropolitan transnational sphere as a woman of colour who

---

[97] *Beyond*, 211. All further references in the text are to this edition.
[98] *Colonialism*, 143.
[99] *Adolescence*.
[100] *Reinvention*, 42.
[101] *Adolescence*. All further references in the text are to this edition.

cannot escape her hybrid identity).

Furthermore, the novel reaffirms, amongst others, Fanon's theory that in a colonial situation "the identity of the colonized [becomes] devaluated, [...] split or conflicted, whereby they may adopt the colonizers' definitions of themselves or absorb colonizers' identities."[102] The author shows how "cultural hybridity causes the individual to be pulled in multiple directions, adopting identities which may differ from one another."[103] The characters of the novel "begin to identify with discourses which may be foreign to [their] own," and are "pulled in multiple directions biologically, physically, and emotionally."[104] The novel demonstrates, quite in Fanon's sense, that, resulting from a continuous exposure to discrimination and oppression, marginalised groups "develop feelings of inferiority, inadequacy, and self-hatred."[105] Hence Tambu's personal story mirrors the entire process that a colonised person goes through, as is outlined in Fanon's theories.[106]

2.3 Trauma and Resistance

Nervous Conditions is certainly a "trauma novel" or, utilising a more general term, a "literature of trauma."[107] Dangarembga describes, explores and analyses the traumatised condition of the colonised and marginalised natives in Rhodesia under the governance of the British Empire. Dangarembga's novel excellently represents most of Ronald Grafonsky's characterisations of trauma literature and thus justly validates its genre. Granofsky argues that (the primary vehicle for the plot in the trauma novel is the search for an integrated, stable identity in the modernist sense). He claims that in the trauma novel the characters' (individual search for identity is inextricably linked to larger social or historical issues), and (the quest for identity in the face of a brutal assault on the sense of self) is often (broken down into three independent 'stages': 'fragmentation,' 'regression,' and 'reunification'). Following his elaboration, the (inassimilable reality) puts the character's (identity under severe stress), and he concludes, (after a painful period of psychic fragmentation, the individual may begin to see a new pattern in things which adumbrates a transformation into an integrated personhood). Moreover, Granof-

---

[102] *Survival*, 39.
[103] *Adolescence.*
[104] *Adolescence.*
[105] *Studies*, 3.
[106] Cp. *Beyond*, 210.
[107] Granofsky, Ronald: *The Trauma Novel: Contemporary Symbolic Depictions of Collective Disaster.* New York: Lang 1995, 5. Hereafter referred to as *Novel*. All further references in the text are to this edition.

sky argues that (the depiction of the trauma novel has some resemblance to what psychiatrists call 'post-traumatic stress disorder' (PTSD)).

PTSD is the psychiatric syndrome that arises out of the experience of trauma, (a psychologically distressing event that is outside the range of usual human experience). PTSD is the response to "an overwhelming experience of sudden or catastrophic events"[108] and describes a number of mental disorders that result from trauma: "reexperiencing symptoms, nightmares, and flashbacks; avoidance symptoms, the marks of psychic numbing; and the symptoms of heightened physiological arousal: hypervigilance, disturbed sleep, a distracted mind."[109] Caruth purports that PTSD "reflects the direct imposition on the mind of the unavoidable reality of horrific events, the taking over of the mind, psychically and neurobiologically, by an event that it cannot control."[110] However, the official diagnosis of the syndrome PTSD and its symptoms are inadequately described as Posttraumatic Stress Disorder (PTSD). I agree with Ashraf Kagee's disapproval of the Western influenced classification of the disorder. PTSD is in colonial and postcolonial contexts certainly not post-traumatic because, as he elucidates, "many people live in communities where the traumatic events continue all the time."[111] He argues that the Western "diagnostic category of post-traumatic stress disorder is probably limited in capturing the experience of people who live under conditions of continuous trauma" and suggests a redefinition of the term into a "continuous traumatic stress disorder."[112] As Fanon himself claimed, "only a psychoanalytic interpretation of the black problem can lay bare the anomalies of affect that are responsible for the structure of the complex."[113] And yet I will refer to it by its proper name since there is no other official definition available yet.

Cathy Caruth and Kai Erikson extend the concept of trauma and PTSD. Caruth adds a historical dimension to PTSD. She argues that PTSD is a pathological symptom of history rather than of the event, for the "traumatised carry an impossible history within them, or they become themselves the symptom of history they cannot entirely

---

[108] *Unclaimed*, 57.
[109] Brown, Laura S.: "Not Outside the Range: One Feminist Perspective on Psychic Trauma." In Cathy Caruth (ed.): *Trauma: Explorations in Memory*. Baltimore: John Hopkins University Press 1995, 100.
[110] *Unclaimed*, 58.
[111] Kagee, Ashraf: "Testing the DSM Model in South Africa." In: Ewald Mengel (ed.): *Trauma, Memory, and Narrative in South Africa: Interviews*. Amsterdam: Rodopi 2010, 129. Hereafter referred to as *Testing*.
[112] *Testing*, 129.
[113] Counihan, Clare: "Reading the Figure of Woman in African Literature: Psychoanalysis, Difference, and Desire." *Research in African Literatures*, 38.2 (2007), 1.

possess."[114] She claims that the symptoms arise not from "a pathology, that is, of falsehood or displacement of meaning, but of history itself."[115] Erikson's sociological approach to trauma provides a reconsideration of the classical definition of trauma and amplifies Caruth's leading position in trauma studies. Erikson's appropriation of the concept of trauma extends the boundaries of its classical definition and is more consistent with colonial trauma. He broadens the concept of trauma by arguing that "in order to serve as a generally useful concept, 'trauma' has to be understood as resulting from a *constellation of life experiences* as well as from a discrete happening, from a *persisting condition* as well as from an acute event."[116] Following his argumentation, trauma shall be extended to the *injury* of the *blow* that inflicted it, and to the *state of mind* that ensues from the *event* that provoked it.[117] Furthermore, he departs from the individual level of trauma and shifts the attention to the collective experience of trauma. By collective trauma, he means

> a blow to the basic tissues of social life that damages the bonds attaching people together and impairs the prevailing sense of communality. The collective trauma works its way slowly and even insidiously into the awareness of those people who suffer from it, so it does not have the quality of suddenness normally associated with "trauma." But it is a form of shock all the same, a gradual realization that the community no longer exists as an effective source of support and that an important part of the self has disappeared.[118]

Erikson's elucidation of collective trauma accurately describes the condition of colonial trauma. Colonialism affects indigenous communities and disrupts their basic structures. As Erikson argues, (when the community is profoundly affected, one can speak of a damaged social organism in almost the same way that one would speak of a damaged body). Thus Erikson renders the wound inflicted on the body into a wound inflicted on the community and validates his extension of trauma concept to a communal level.

Dangarembga's exploration of trauma, similarly to Erikson's description of communal trauma, portrays the (damage to the tissues that hold human groups intact) brought about by the colonial system. The novel explores how colonialism inflicts damage to the (creation of social climates) and disrupts (communal moods, that come to dominate a group's spirit). The novel also reveals the historical dimension of trauma

---

114 Caruth, Cathy (ed.): *Trauma: Explorations in Memory*. Baltimore: John Hopkins University Press 1995, 5. Hereafter referred to as *Trauma*.
115 *Trauma*, 5.
116 Erikson, Kai: "Notes on Trauma and Community." In: Cathy Caruth (ed.): *Trauma: Explorations in Memory*. Baltimore: John Hopkins University Press 1995, 185. Hereafter referred to as *Community*.
117 *Community*, 184.
118 *Community*, 187. All further references in the text are to this edition.

and its symptoms. The novelist discloses the history of colonialism that is responsible for the psychic ruptures and traumas of the marginalised native population. The traumatised natives become the symptoms of history they cannot assimilate. It is the colonial history of injustice and oppression that they cannot integrate into their indigenous repertoire of common sense. Dangarembga's highly self-reflexive trauma novel depicts the nervous conditions of its characters that result from living in a continuously traumatising colonial environment, and delineates the symptoms inherent to the experience of trauma. Moreover, she challenges Fanon and expands his work by providing solutions and issues he leaves unexplored. In this chapter I will explore the traumas of the characters of the novel, their respective reactions and symptoms, and their possible resistance.

2.3.1 The Trauma of Colonisation

The first event in the novel that can be classified as an instance of post-traumatic stress disorder (PTSD) is Tambu's nightmare about her lately deceased brother Nhamo. When Tambu spends her first night at the mission she dreams of him and is plagued by guilt. Tambu relates:

> The dream became a nightmare [...] Nhamo howled with a vicious glee, telling me that I would come to a bad end, that I deserved it for deserting my husband, my children, my garden and my chickens. He spoke with such authority that I was ashamed of deserting this family that I did not have. (91)

The nightmare suggests Tambu's feelings of guilt about taking Nhamo's place at the mission. In the dream he blames her for deserting her future obligations as a woman. Nhamo's image as a proponent of patriarchy reappears and haunts her in the nightmare. Before Nhamo died, Tambu was deeply hurt when she realised that he partook in the justification of the social inequality which aimed at keeping "women as exclusive child-rearers."[119] Tambu's nightmare is one of the symptoms of PTSD and relates "to the ways in which 'the traumatic event is persistently re-experienced'."[120] Tambu's relocation to the mission can be read as a stressor which activates and relieves the sensory experience of the traumatising event. On her first day at the mission she compares Nhamo's description of Babamukuru's house with her own perception of it. The situation reminds her that her brother was there before he died and now she is about to

---

[119] *Survival*, 50.
[120] *Question*, 1.

take her place at the mission.

In the context of colonial trauma, Nhamo's death can be interpreted as a tragic outcome of his nervous condition. His mother, Mainini, frequently refers to the deathly consequences of 'Englishness' if one is not careful. Mainini regularly blames Babamukuru and his wife for Nhamo's death: "You and your education have killed my son" (54). Symbolically speaking, she blames Englishness for his death. Mainini warns Tambu not to follow in Nhamo's footsteps, "The problem is the Englishness, so you just be careful!" (207). As Erikson suggests, it makes sense to conclude that Mainini's "traumatized view of the world conveys a wisdom that ought to be heard in its own terms."[121] Moreover, the missing evidence for the cause of his premature death leaves a possibility open for a connection between his death and Englishness. The novel never reveals the exact cause of his death. Tambu remembers, "Now, we did not know whether the departed has suffered from mumps or not... Anyway, the doctor was not sure" (55). This statement signals that he did not necessarily die from mumps and that it could have been something else. Moreover, Tambu summarises the load of future responsibility Nhamo's would have had to shoulder: "Nhamo knew a lot of things in those days. He knew that it would be up to him to make sure that his younger sisters were educated, or look after us if we were not" (15). The burden of responsibility and obligations alludes to his nervous condition as he takes up his education at the mission.

In the course of the novel Tambu shows several symptoms of trauma correlated to events which remind her of her trauma and activate traumatic stressors. In such moments "the food would not go down" (93). Tambu describes an unpleasant symptom: "a horrible crawling over my skin, my chest contracted to a breathless tension and even my bowels threatened to let me know their opinion" (151). After Babamukuru's and Nyasha's fight, where they were literally "out for each other's blood" (115), and when Babamukuru called his daughter "a whore" (116) for her inappropriate British behaviour, Tambu realises the universal female victimisation. The realisation induces her remembrance of the unfair treatment based on her femaleness by her father and deceased brother. In an attempt to escape the unbearable thoughts, she takes "refuge in the image of the grateful poor relative" (118) and refuses to think about her traumatic past experience. She says, "I didn't want to explore the treacherous mazes that such thoughts led into" (118). This avoidance behaviour is symptomatic of PTSD. Tambu attempts to escape the stimuli associated with her trauma of gender inequalities, but the symptoms

---

[121] *Community*, 198.

accumulate and lead to "her main symptom," "a kind of paralysis that follows from repression."[122]

The severity of Tambu's traumatised condition comes to light at the advent of her parents' Christian wedding. When her uncle insists on the immediate need for the wedding to take place, Tambu experiences an immense nervous condition which intensifies her trauma. It is the impossibility to negotiate between the two ideologies, between the Shona tradition and Christianity, that she finds so disturbing. Tambu is split between the knowledge about sin she acquired in school and the traditions of her people. It comes as a shock to her when she realises the absurdity of the whole proce-dure. The wedding scene introduces Tambu's major trauma in the novel. The wedding is so dramatic for Tambu because it disrupts her basic beliefs. Her parents' wedding challenges Tambu's unquestioned assumptions about herself and the world. The wedding ceremony represents a major violation of Tambu's core beliefs and threatens to completely undermine the bedrock on which Tambu grounds her existence.[123] Tambu's psychic trauma results "from the processes involved in dealing with (rejecting, accom-modating, or integrating) the new information into existing belief structures."[124] Tambu's attempt to integrate the wedding ceremony into her belief system fails due to the inconsistency of the two cultures in such a delicate case. Tambu's doubt about her legitimate existence shatters her basic beliefs, which "are postulated to be fundamental to psychological health."[125] The wedding is meant to legitimise the long union of her parents, which means that they have lived in sin and she is the product of that illegal union, in Christian terms. The traumatic event upsets her basic beliefs and causes considerable emotional disturbance. She says, "To me the question of that wedding was a serious one, so serious that even my body reacted in a very alarming way" (151). Tambu blames her uncle for initiating a ceremony that "made such a joke of [her] parents, [her] home and [herself]" (151). In spite of her conviction that the wedding makes a mockery of her parents, she cannot speak her mind to Babmukuru. Thinking or talking about trauma means the traumatised is exposed to the unbearable events. Tambu's "avoidance of stimuli associated with the trauma" is expressed in her "avoid-ance of thoughts."[126] She says: "Thoughts of the wedding were not allowed to linger in

---

[122] *Reinvention*, 44.
[123] Cp. Bower, Gordon H., Heidi Sivers: "Cognitive Impact of Traumatic Events." *Development and Psychopathology: Risk, Trauma, Memory*, 10.4 (1998), 645. Hereafter referred to as *Cognitive*.
[124] *Cognitive*, 645.
[125] *Cognitive*, 646.
[126] *Question*, 1.

my mind since they had such serious, sinful consequences. To distract myself I set my mind on other things" (151). Nonetheless her split mind cannot rest from the matter. She says: "But the advantages and disadvantages of the white lace and vows and veils at this late stage battled about in my head so furiously that I could not sleep for nights on end" (166). She feels guilty about her inability to make a stand against the ridiculous ceremony and lets "guilt, so many razor-sharp edges of it slice away at [her]" (167).

On the morning of the wedding Tambu cannot get out of her bed. She is paralysed. She says, "I tried several times but my muscles simply refused to obey" (168). Her numbing is one of the symptoms of PTSD. Tambu describes her experience as follows: "I was slipping further and further away [...] until in the end I appeared to have slipped out of my body and was standing somewhere near the foot of the bed, watching [...]" (168). Tambu's condition can be referred to as dissociation. Dissociation "is closely linked with trauma" and "is viewed as an adaptive response to overwhelming and inescapable threat or trauma."[127] Dissociation as a frequent accompaniment of trauma happens when "the victim experiences a disruption in self."[128] Pierre Janet believes that at the heart of this psychopathology lies a lack of integration, or 'dissociation', of unusual experiences.[129] The mental pathology "is characterized by the victim having subjective experiences of emotional numbing, derealization, depersonalization, and perceptual alterations during the trauma."[130] Tambu's depiction of dissociation is reminiscent of the description provided by Gordon H. Bower and Heidi Sivers. They state that the affected person reports "that he or she 'spaces out,' feels 'unreal,' and perceives events as strange and distant, as though they were not really happening to him or her."[131] Tambu says: "I heard [Babamukuru and Nyasha] talking from a great distance that rapidly diminished as I slipped back into my body" (169).

---

[127] Antze, Paul et al. (ed.): *Tense Past: Cultural Essays in Trauma and Memory*. New York: Routledge 1996, 179. Hereafter referred to as *Tense*.
[128] *Cognitive*, 641.
[129] Cp. *Cognitive*, 641.
[130] *Cognitive*, 641.
[131] *Cognitive*, 641.

2.3.2 Tambu's Resistance

It is only after her dissociative state of mind that Tambu finally finds herself capable of uttering her reluctance to attend the wedding. She resists her uncle's plan to be her mother's bridesmaid at the wedding. Tambu eventually finds her voice and is able to make up her mind. She states, "I'm sorry, Babamukuru, but I do not want to go to the wedding" (169), and proclaims: "I had made my decision and the decision at least was mine" (171). Thus she is finally able to take "a stand against superimposing inappropriate Western religious ideas upon Shona marriage traditions."[132] With the scene, the narrator illustrates "how her absence from the wedding signifies a point of conscious withdrawal from patriarchal order."[133] Moreover, it helps her to arrange her split thoughts and establish her "newly acquired identity" (171). Thus the symptoms of PTSD also have a positive effect in relation to colonial resistance. As Sugnet underlines, "the symptom is itself a kind of resistance, an involuntary inability to succumb completely to oppression."[134] Her resistance and unwillingness to attend the wedding signals her rootedness in Shona culture. Her respect for Shona traditions implies that she has maintained her cultural traditions and has not wholly succumbed to assimilation.

With Tambu's acquisition of her new identity after the occurrence of dissociation, Dangarembga challenges Fanon. She is able to provide a concrete solution for Fanon's implied revolutionary consciousness that is needed for resistance to colonialism. Through Nyasha's lessons on oppression and discrimination Tambu develops a "sort of revolutionary consciousness" that "Fanon leaves implicit" in *The Wretched of the Earth*.[135] In the course of the novel, Nyasha's warnings and critical evaluation of the colonial condition provide Tambu with a critical apparatus that problematises her "adherence to the white model of success and thereby 'ruins Tambu's linear plans for education and for a clear-cut, wholly unambiguous sense of identity'."[136] Nyasha functions as a supportive character and an initiator for Tambu's re-examination of "the identity she has been seeking for herself away from her family's homestead."[137] Tambu's initial disapproval of her anglicised cousin for her lack of decorum alters to admiration of her ability to "pluck out the heart of a problem with her multidirectional mind and present it to [her] in ways that made sense" (153). Under Nyasha's tutelage, Tambu develops the

---

[132] *Negotiating*, 72.
[133] *Adolescence*, 4.
[134] *Reinvention*, 45.
[135] *Collusions*, 18, 20.
[136] *Beyond*, 212.
[137] *Beyond*, 212.

ability to query the discrepancies of her being she previously tried to ignore. Her cousin triggers a sort of revolution of her consciousness when she critically analyses the colonial condition, "'It's bad enough,' [...] 'when a country gets colonised, but when the people do as well! That's the end, really, that's the end'" (150). Nyasha warns Tambu about her education at Sacred Heart, "there [are] more evils than advantages to be reaped from such an opportunity. It would be a marvellous opportunity [...] to forget. To forget who you were, what you were and why you were that" (182). Tambu eventually accepts the thoughts she repeatedly pushed aside, "preferring to pursue without question an unexamined life committed to educational advancement."[138]

The close of the novel reveals that Tambu has taken her cousin's lessons and her mother's repetitive warnings about colonial domination and oppression seriously. Tambu seems to have found her new identity in (the doubleness of her existence). Though she is (never able to secure an absolute position on one or the other side of the divide), and therefore (still occupies that same ambiguous space [that] Fanon predicted for the psyche of the colonized person), she is able to find the resolution Fanon leaves open in his work. Tambu "arrives at a sense of her own agency"[139] by finding her way of coping with the ambiguous situation. She develops the ability to filter and resist the unmitigated influence of colonial hegemony. After a long quest throughout the novel she finally arrives at the conclusion to make the best of her Western education but simultaneously never to forget her African ancestry. In the closing paragraph of "the text, the *bildungsroman*, or novel of development,"[140] she states,

> Although I was not aware of it then, no longer could I accept Sacred Heart and what it represented as a sunrise on my horizon. [...] something in my mind began to assert itself, to question things and refuse to be brainwashed. [...] It was a long and painful process for me, that process of expansion. (208)

Tambu finds a way in-between, a key to her survival in a changing society and a path for resistance to the obliteration of her African identity.

---

[138] *Beyond*, 212.
[139] *Collusions*, 19.
[140] *Collusions*, 19.

2.3.3 Nyasha's Resistance

Another symptom of trauma and resistance is expressed through Nyasha's illness, bulimia or anorexia nervosa. Her chronic suffering brought about by the colonial condition takes the shape of her acute illness. Nyaha's illness is the consequence of "the most obvious and quintessential 'nervous condition' in the novel."[141] Her hybridity and desperate rebellion against her father over gaining control over her own body and femininity leads to her suffering. Nyasha's inability to assert herself in colonial Rhodesia leads to her desperate attempts to gain control over the only thing she still possesses, her own fragile female body. In her astute analysis of the whole situation in the novel she blames the colonial system for her suffering of not belonging. Nyasha says to Tambu, "It is not really him [Babamukuru], you know. I mean not really the person. It's everything, it's everywhere. So where do you break out to?" (176). Her situation causes a perpetual harm to her soul and mind. Sugnet argues that her illness provides "the imagery of eating, digestion, nutrition, vomiting, and excerption" which are "crucial metaphors for domination and resistance in the novel."[142] She figuratively vomits out the colonialism of which she ate too much. Tambu's mother makes frequent comments on eating in relation to colonialism as well. She warns Tambu to not digest too much of British culture: "You couldn't expect the ancestors to stomach so mush Englishness" (207). Eating disturbances are also described in Fanon's *The Wretched of the Earth*. Fanon reports cases when victims suffer from "loss of appetite arising from mental causes" and "patients who will not eat and explode with hostility when touched."[143] Remarkably, "he uses the term 'anorexia' to describe the cases."[144] Moreover, eating disturbances are among the symptoms of PTSD.

Towards the close of the novel Nyasha's state assumes a dramatic shape, of not only doubtfulness about her survival from anorexia nervosa but also her strained mental condition. After Tambu's three months absence, she returns from the convent school to spend her holidays on the mission. What she faces there is "a horribly weird and sinister drama" (202). Nyasha has grown skeletal and advances her illness. Tambu reports that she "shovelled the food into her mouth, swallowing without chewing and without pause" and vomited it immediately thereafter in the bathroom (202). Tambu describes her skeletal body, "her bony knees pressed together so that her nightdress fell through

---

[141] *Reinvention*, 35.
[142] *Reinvention*, 35.
[143] *Reinvention*, 35.
[144] *Reinvention*, 35.

the space where her tights had been" (204). In a catastrophic scene of Nyasha's mental and violent rage she accuses colonialism for her affliction. There she speaks in several different voices. Tambu notes: "Her voice took on a Rhodesian accent. Then she was whispering again. … she said softly. … she said in a voice that was recognisably hers" (205). She also changes her behaviour during the outbreak: "She began to rock; she raged and crouched like a cat ready to spring; she rampaged, shedding her history book between her teeth, breaking mirrors; she curled up in Maiguru's lap looking no more than five years old" (205). The description of her outbreak is symptomatic of Dissociative Identity Disorder (formerly called Multiple Personality Disorder)—"an involuntary and somewhat uncanny alteration of personal identities accompanied by amnesic episodes."[145] The description is indicative of "dissociative experiences—as shifts in mental state or changes in voice."[146] In her rage she easily moves from one state to another. Nyasha's dissociative identity disorder is the result of her trauma, which can be read as "a cascade of experiences, eruptions, crevasses, a sliding of tectonic plates that undergird the self."[147] Nyasha's mental and physical illness is the tragic result of "her anger and feelings of being trapped," and a system that makes her into "a victim of her femaleness."[148] In addition, her speaking in several different voices resonates with the political and social upheavals of colonialism. Zwicker argues that at that moment Nyasha becomes "a cipher for the confusion of ideologies and locations marked out in a period of intense social destabilization."[149]

Moreover, Nyasha's anorexia or bulimia nervosa represents the violence Fanon referred to in his *The Wretched of the Earth*. According to his ideas, (colonialism is inherently violent" and because it is "violent, it breeds a violent response). Zwicker argues that "Nyasha figures the very dialectic of colonial and anti-colonial violence that Fanon suggests" in his work, and that she (is the clearest object of the warning implied in the novel's title and epigraph). Her eating disorder lucidly echoes the "nervous condition" of the title.[150] Shatteman notes that Nyasha's rage as she tears up her history book and screams, "I won't grovel, I won't die" (205), is in fact one possible response to the anxiety brought on by the socio-political climate of the country.[151] Moreover, her rage illustrates "the angry defence of blackness" implied by Fanon's *Black Skin, White*

---

[145] *Tense*, 152.
[146] *Tense*, 180.
[147] *Tense*, 181.
[148] *Negotiating*, 74.
[149] Collusions, 17. All further references in the text are to this edition.
[150] Cp. *Collusions*, 17.
[151] Cp. *Beyond*, 210.

Masks.[152] I disagree with Zwicker's opinion that Nyasha gives her consent to her nervous condition as implied by Satre and omitted by Dangarembga in the prologue of the book. Zwicker approves of the interpretation that Nyasha is complicit in her colonisation and argues that her "anorexia suggests a degree of agency in the form of consent."[153] Differently from other characters, she does not willingly participate in her colonisation. Since she was taken by force to England her hybridity is performed unconsciously, and she spots the disadvantages of colonial privileges in her astute analysis of the whole situation. Therefore, Nyasha materialises Fanon's arguments as read by Satre only with respect to her violent response. Her response to colonisation in the form of her violent anti-colonial struggle against literal and figurative domination is a willed act.[154]

Furthermore, Fanon's second term is that "violence is not only destructive, but also creative," in that "it produces national identity."[155] However, the second term does not apply in Nyasha's case as it does in Tambu's. Nyasha's early uprootedness impedes the development of national identity in her and makes her body figuratively and literally into the battleground on which the violent response to colonisation and domination takes place. The novel suggests that her agency may not take Nyasha very far insofar as she ends up weakened and sick.[156] The last word the narrator gives us on Nyasha is that "progress was still in the balance" (206).

Nyasha's predicament, read through Fanon, reveals her paradoxical situation. Zwicker argues that on the one hand she is the intellectual Fanon requires for resistance, for an intellectual, in Fanon's words, "teach[es] the masses that everything depends on them."[157] But on the other hand, cut off "from maintaining meaningful relationships" with her people, Nyasha's intellectual path of teaching Tambu "on thinking [in] revolutionary national thoughts" is shown to be only "self-destructive."[158]

2.3.4 The Female Empowerment and Conclusion

Other women of the novel also show signs of mental illness and resistance. Mainini, who is feeling helpless and worn out by the weight of poverty and childbearing,

---

[152] *Beyond*, 210.
[153] *Collusions*, 17.
[154] Cp. *Collusions*, 18.
[155] *Collusions*, 10.
[156] Cp. *Collusions*, 18.
[157] *Collusions*, 19.
[158] *Collusions*, 19.

succumbs to depression after her daughter's admittance to the Roman Catholic Convent School. However, her depression is not a sudden reaction to the fear of losing her daughter to British culture, but an aggravation of her prior fears. A week before Tambu's departure for the mission school, Mainini's anxiety spoils her appetite: "she ate hardly anything" and "she could hardly walk to the fields, let alone work in them" (57). When Tambu visits her parents in the Christmas holidays, she finds her pregnant mother in a bad condition even though her body seems to be unaffected. Tambu relates, "she was not looking ill at all. In fact, she was looking much stronger than she had been when I last saw her" (133). Tambu reports that Mainini suffers from "unlocalised aches all over her body" (131). Her suffering discloses the symptoms of the illness of the soul associated with trauma. After Tambu wins a scholarship and is thrilled to start her education at the white convent school, Mainini sees the validation of her concerns of loosing Tambu to white culture. She develops depression and stops eating and looking after her baby: "She ate less and less and did less and less, within days she could neither eat nor do anything, not even change the dress she wore....reacting to nothing" (187). Mainini's depression is likely to be attributed to the anxiety disorder of PTSD, after her exposure to multiple traumatic experiences of first losing her son to 'Englishness' and then the immediate threat of losing her daughter the same way. Her younger sister Lucia's "shock treatment" (188) brings her back to washing herself and looking after her baby. Her sister's help in caring for her baby relieves at least for a while the weight of Mainini's motherhood. Moreover, with her early insights into the dangers of 'Englishness', Mainini "is the first to actually recognize Nyasha's eating disorder, and to diagnose it: 'It's Englishness,' [207] she says shortly."[159] Zwicker contends that Tambu's mother "sees things more clearly than do other characters of the text," and therefore, she "demonstrates an extraordinary self-consciousness throughout the novel."[160]

Dangarembga brings up the issue of the voice of subaltern woman in the novel, left ignored by Fanon. She not only challenges Fanon by emphasising the importance of gender in colonial discourse, but also eradicates the voicelessness of the subaltern woman by giving her a voice in her novel. Maiguru finds a way to resist the patriarchal dominance of her mighty husband and succeeds in finding her voice in the novel. Dangarembga depicts the "strained atmosphere" of "the homestead and the mission,"[161]

---

[159] *Collusions*, 20.
[160] *Collusions*, 20.
[161] *Beyond*, 210.

where Maiguru is "hysterically over compliant with Shona patriarchal expectations" in spite of her "excellent education."[162] The tense situation makes her "sick" (174) from supporting Babamukuru's family financially and physically and being permanently silenced by her husband. She complains of being unnerved by "the inmates of her house" (115). Finally she escapes her miserable nervous condition and flees from her husband's house. After her "five-day hiatus"[163] she changes her attitude and returns as a confident woman. She loses most of her "baby-talk" (178) and no longer calls her husband "her Daddy-sweet" (166). Tambu talks about the difference: "She smiled more often and less mechanically, fussed over us less and was more willing or able to talk about sensible things" (178).

With the novel, the author demonstrates "*gendered* contexts" of predicament and resistance and makes "visible a range of responses to oppressive situations."[164] The novel tells a story about the resistance of colonised African women. It reveals "how Zimbabwean women can find collective and personal voices in a patriarchal society suffering from the effects of colonization."[165] The novelist stresses that the resistance emanates from the women in the novel. On the one hand, the novel is a double critique of colonialism and sexism, but on the other hand, it concedes a subtle glorification of women's oppression. In the long run women even benefit from it to some degree because they are less affected by assimilation. Since native women are less exposed to the dangers of colonial rule, they are less traumatised. Even though the author explicitly criticises women's degradation and their deprivation of the right and opportunity to belong to the colonial elite, she exposes women's better point of departure to cope with Englishness than that of men. Dangarembga's novel implies that the doubly colonised women are better off because they are more likely to generate a resistance. The men in the novel are excluded from showing such acute symptoms of resistance due to their direct inclusion in the centre of colonial hegemony. Men are more directly subjected to colonial influence and, as agents of the implementation of the colonial system, they are more directly affected and thus endangered by Englishness. Their closeness to the centre makes them accomplices of their colonial masters and leaves less space for resistance. Since they are further away from the centre of the system, women's "symp-

---

[162] *Negotiating*, 74.
[163] *Collusions*, 20.
[164] *Collusions*, 21.
[165] *Literature*, 102.

toms are likely to be expressed more fully and disruptively."[166]

Furthermore, with the book, the author creates an empowering act of self-assertion and "arrives at a sense of her own agency."[167] The author makes use of "the tools given by colonial education to make her own account of herself." [168] Paradoxically, the means she employs to articulate her consciousness and resistance are provided by the system she is criticising. Her work demonstrates that she has learnt to take advantage of colonial education in order to break out of silence and reclaim agency for herself. The plot of the novel demonstrates how she finds her own agency to combat the unjust system, and the novel itself is the evidence to her resistance. In the novel, she captures the traditions and rituals of her people in the language of the system that sought to extinguish them. With her account she shows that stomaching some 'Englishness' is ultimately empowering.[169] Thus she writes back to the canon, and lays bare the complexities of the psyche of the colonised. She clarifies the continuous nature of colonial trauma and elucidates the consequences of living in a system woven with injustice and oppression. The novel illustrates how the women's attitudes change and they find their voice and thus the means of articulation for their opinion. Dangarembga shows that the symptoms of colonial trauma also have a positive meaning. They are hints of resistance to subjugation, injustice and silencing. Therefore, the symptom of resistance is "a curse, but it is also a blessing."[170] Dangaremba leaves the ending open and never tells us what will become of anorexic Nyasha. Nyasha, left still alive and struggling, leaves a chance open for healing and survival. Though the formerly colonised subject will never get back to his or her pre-colonial state, he or she can survive carrying the scars of his or her colonial past. Similarly, Nyasha might recuperate but never become fully unaffected, like Tambu, who certainly does survive with the trauma of the past lingering in her soul.

Dangarembga's novel is an act of resistance to colonial oppression and has an alleviating effect on the author. Similarly to her main character, she "finds self and communal articulation through writing."[171] The novel reclaims what has been stolen by colonialism and is an act of assertion of the rights and traditions of the indigenous population. Zwicker notes that the author "self-consciously crafts a national literature

---

[166] *Reinvention*, 45.
[167] *Collusions*, 19.
[168] *Reinvention*, 47.
[169] Cp. *Reinvention*, 45.
[170] *Reinvention*, 45.
[171] *Collusions*, 20.

42

for the new Zimbabwe—a national literature that puts young women first."[172] In addition, the book suggests Dangarembga's objection to the traditional thinking in binary oppositions and implies following historical changes and integrating a new, third term of in-betweenness. Moreover, with the novel, Dangarembga comes to terms with her unnatural rejection of her deceased brother Nhamo. On the whole, although "the novel opens with Nhamo's death and ends with Nyasha's near-death,"[173] Dangarembga's goal is not to depict violence but to emphasise resistance. The narrator Tambudzai, or Tambu, states in the opening of the book, "my story is not after all about death, but about my escape and Lucia's; about my mother's and Maiguru's entrapment; and about Nyasha's rebellion" (1).

---

[172] *Collusions*, 21.
[173] *Collusions*, 13.

3. *Kiss of the Fur Queen*

3.1 The Question of Identity

Tomson Highway's semi-autobiographical novel *Kiss of the Fur Queen* "is based on the events that lead to his brother René's death of AIDS."[174] Tomson Highway, born in 1951 in northern Manitoba, is a Cree writer and Residential School survivor. He is a two-time winner of the Dora Mavor Moore Award for his plays.[175] *Kiss of the Fur Queen* is the first and only novel of Canada's best known and most talented native playwright. The novel "explores the tormented relationship between the Canadian Catholic church and a Native community in the Canadian north."[176] It focuses on the atrocities suffered by the two Cree brothers, Champion-Jeremiah and Ooneemeetoo-Gabriel, in the fictional Birch Lake Residential School in Northern Manitoba. Champion-Jeremiah is sent to the Birch Lake Residential School after seven joyful years with his family, joined two years later by his younger brother Ooneemeetoo-Gabriel. At the Catholic boarding school the two young brothers are gradually estranged from their Cree roots and their native identity. The boys are regularly sexually abused by their care-takers, the Catholic priests. The author presents their life following the abuse, which is badly marked by the traumatising experience.

Highway portrays the boys' childhood trauma of dislocation and deprivation of familial love and care, and the horrors of sexual abuse. The enforced civilisation and assimilation of the Cree brothers mirrors "one of the most efficient tools" of the European expansion in Canada to "kill the Indian in the Indian."[177] The disruption of parent-child bonds and a "systematic destruction of traditional Indian family struc-tures"[178] is essential for the rupture of their Native identity. The deprivation of harmo-nious parental bonds, "traditionally regarded as pivotal for the development of a [healthy] personality and the basis for the human capacity to relate to others,"[179] is symptomatic of the protagonists' identity and relational problems. Highway's novel

---

[174] Athabasca University. 2011. "Tomson Highway." *English-Canadian Writers*.
   <http://www.athabascau.ca/cll/writers/english/writers/thighway/thighway.php> (03.06.2012).
   Hereafter referred to as *Writers*.
[175] Cp. *Writers*.
[176] Hogeterp-Koopman, Jane: "Bhabha, the Trickster and the Church: Re-viewing Canda's Post-Colonial Present." In: Deborah E. Bowen (ed.): *The Strategic Smorgasbord of Postmodernity: Literature and the Christian Critic*. Newcastle: Cambridge Scholars Publishing 2007, 196. Hereafter referred to as *Trickster*.
[177] Klein, Verena: "Healing the Native Canadian Soul: Three Accounts of Spiritual Homecoming." *Litteraria Pragensia: Studies in Literature and Culture*, 15.30 (2005), 37. Hereafter referred to as *Homecoming*.
[178] *Homecoming*, 43.
[179] *Homecoming*, 43.

captures the grim atmosphere of the Christian Residential Schools, where Aboriginal children were separated "from their families and as a consequence from their language, culture and religious beliefs."[180] Representing the fate of thousands of Aboriginal children, the novelist displays the Cree brothers' physical and mental abuse, and also their suffering at the hands of the Catholic priests of the boarding school.

The novel depicts the victimisation of Canada's First Nations as a consequence of the colonists' steady expansion and increasing need for land to cultivate. The Indians were forced to live in designated areas because their "traditional nomadic way of life was considered an obstacle"[181] to the Europeans' economic interests in land and agriculture. These Indian reservations were gradually civilised by Canada's Catholic missionaries. The author explores the identity formation in a rapidly changing world of colonial and postcolonial conditions (though Canada officially gained its independence from Britain in 1931, technically and formally it lasted until 1982). He delineates the process of the deconstruction of Native identity and explores the intricate process of the formation of hybrid identity. Highway reconstructs "the inevitably hybridized identities of contemporary First Nations people"[182] based on his own biography. Hence, based on his protagonists, he explores his own identity. His distraught protagonists are torn between the binary oppositions of the two cultures. Their unstable identities are always in a constant flux of negotiation and reformation of the 'self'. Their selves are always shifting between Nativity and Westernisation, between essence and desire, between tradition and modernisation, in a constant search for the true self.

The constant negotiation of identity formation is one of the main themes in the novel. Highway's semi-omniscient narrator calls the main protagonist of the novel, Jeremiah Okimasis, either by his Cree or his Christian name, or a combination of both, expressing closeness or distance to his Indian heritage.[183] The novel illustrates the brothers' childhood traumas and "terrors of the Roman Catholic Residential School three hundred miles from home which they are forced by law to attend, in order to be educated white."[184] The early separation from parents and family and a sudden relocation to an unfamiliar establishment with strict rules and incomprehensible demands causes great harm to the souls of the young boys. The sudden break abruptly ends "the

---

[180] *Homecoming*, 37.
[181] *Homecoming*, 37.
[182] Howells, Coral Ann: "Tomson Highway: 'Kiss of the Fur Queen'." In: Coral Ann Howells (ed.): *Where are the Voices Coming From? Canadian Culture and the Legacies of History*. Amsterdam: Rodopi 2004, 84. Hereafter referred to as *Queen*.
[183] *Homecoming*, 39.
[184] *Queen*, 87.

brothers' idyllic early childhood in their native village of Eemanapiteepitat."[185] The enforced denial of their Native Cree identity initiates the brothers' traumatic condition in the novel.

3.1.1 Acculturation

Highway shows the effects of cultural alienation and forced assimilation on his main protagonist, Jeremiah Okimasis, who embodies the author in the novel. In the novel, Jeremiah illustrates the beginning of Christianisation of his land: "1860. The first missionary arrives on Mistik Lake" (291). The Christianisation reaches his Native Indian reservation at the time when his younger brother Gabriel is born: "A mere two hundred yards south of the Okimasis cabin, [...] the priest in his study, a nail in one hand, a hammer in the other, poise[s] to nail a brand-new crucifix into a wall" (17). The narrator depicts the rapid progress of the government's intervention in the reservation: "Eemanapiteepitat now attacked the plane en masse, for ever since the first [airplane] had landed on Mistik Lake in 1929, the population had never been able to resist swarming" (188). Symbolised by the nail and hammer as the missionary's instruments of torment, the narrator depicts the forced conversion of his people. Following the government's policy of the obliteration of Indian culture, the priest orders the Indians to stop their dancing activities on the reservation: "No good Catholic danced on Sundays, Father Eustache Bouchard had told his flock repeatedly" (17).

A significant tool tor the implementation of the government's assimilation policy was to separate Indian children from their families. The author exposes the process of the "complication of Native identity, initiated by Residential Schooling."[186] The protagonists' state of split selves is preceded by the splitting of their family. Highway points at the parents' distress at "the thought of losing Champion to boarding school" (43). Jeremiah's mother, Mariesis Okimasis, shows her dissatisfaction at the prospect of losing her son to the "school in the south" (40). She is "frightened" and "want[s] to cry" (42). His father, Abraham Okimasis, deplores "the law" of the Department of Indian Affairs, "wishing dearly that he had some say in the matter" (40). Feeling powerless and robbed of his parental right to decide for his children, he reassures his wife "that he, at least, would never leave her" (42). The parents' distress shows how the process meant

---

[185] *Queen*, 87.
[186] McKegney, Sam: "Claiming Narrative Control: Tomson Highway on Residential Schooling." *Culture and the State: Disability Studies & Indigenous Studies,* 2003, 67. Hereafter referred to as *Control*.

to disrupt the intergenerational passing on of Native identity destroys the balance within the traditional Cree family.

The most striking illustration of the children's forced identity negation is the change of Champion's Cree name. The priests of the Catholic school despotically change his Aboriginal name into a Christian one, thereby enforcing upon him a Christian identity against his wishes. By depriving him of his Cree name, the priest symbolically erodes his Aboriginal identity. Champion is renamed Jeremiah right after his arrival from the Eemanapiteepitat reservation. His younger brother Ooneemeetoo (Dancer) is renamed Gabriel as early as the baptism ceremony. The infant's godmother, Annie Moostoos, struggles to prevent the renaming of "her two week old ... godson" (36). She implores Father Bouchard, a "priest and missionary *extraordinaire*" (36) to keep the boy's Cree name. She begs, "'But he already has a name,' ... 'His name,' she state[s] 'is Ooneemeetoo. Ooneemeetoo Okimasis'" (37). The narrator echoes the infant's forced renaming by the priest's instrument of subjugation and torment: "'Gabriel Okimasis,' the oblate state[s], as if *to nail* 'Gabriel' permanently" (37, emphasis mine).

The enforcement of the Christian names is emblematic of Canada's policy of "aggressive civilization" and "forced assimilation."[187] Residential Schools endeavoured to Christianise Canada's First Nations, and thereby "to destroy Native cultures by altering Native identity among the young."[188] For over a century the Canadian government attempted to (get rid of the Indian problem) through the coercive acculturation of indigenous youth in the Residential School system. The (culturally genocidal objective) was intended (to continue until there is not a single Indian in Canada that has not been absorbed into the body politic, and there is no Indian question, and no Indian Department).

Additionally to the renaming, another infamous practice of forced civilisation involved cutting off the Indians' traditionally long hair. Highway depicts the suffering of his young protagonists as they get "shorn of their hair, their Indian names and identities."[189] The Cree brothers get their hair cut upon their arrival. The cutting off of their hair portrays the destruction of the brothers' Cree identity. In the humiliating scene Champion loses his hair and is renamed by Father Lafleur. When Champion approaches

---

[187] *Homecoming*, 37.
[188] *Control*, 66. All further references in the text are to this edition.
[189] *Queen*, 87.

the hairdresser he feels "poised for the slaughter" and has to call "forth every ounce of courage so he wouldn't burst into tears" (52). When his hair is being cut, he feels as if "he [is] being skinned alive, in public; the centre of his nakedness shrivel[s] to the size and texture of a raisin, the whole world staring, pointing, laughing" (53). The duality of the erosion of his identity, namely the extinction of his Cree name and the traditionally long hair, severely afflicts his state of mind: "Champion fe[els] the tear that, against his best intentions, [...] escape[s] from his right eye. [...] His hair now gone completely, Champion ha[s] no strength left; he beg[ins] to bawl" (54). The scene demonstrates the boy's anguish as he experiences a literal mutilation of the core of his Aboriginal identity.

Another practice of the coerced acculturation was the "forced speaking of non-native languages."[190] The novel illustrates the Native language ban. Upon arrival in the Residential School, the Okimasis brothers have no command of English and are forbidden to speak their own language. Jeremiah is instructed by Father Lafleur, the principal of the school: "Now, Jeremiah. You know you're not to speak Cree once you're off the plane" (70). The ban against speaking Cree at school is augmented by a competition which awards a monthly prize to those students who catch the greatest number of pupils speaking Cree: Champion-Jeremiah's "Cree must not be heard or he would fail to win the prize" (63). The competition is meant "to guarantee the Indian children's continuous use of English," the consequence being that, "after several years at the school the brothers lose their capacity to communicate fluently in Cree."[191] Furthermore, the boys are frequently punished by the priests when caught speaking Cree: "Gabriel's crime had been to be caught singing 'Kimoosoom Chimasoo'" (85).

3.1.2 Christianisation

The Okimasis brothers' introduction into white culture entails an initiation of the doubleness of their identity, detectable in the ambiguity and splitting of identity. Highway reveals the role of the Catholic Church in the engenderment of ambivalence. The author illustrates the failures of the Christian Church to convey the principal virtues of the faith to their young Indian subjects. He shows that rather than teaching the pupils about Christian beliefs, the missionaries "discredit[...] and obscure[...] Christianity."[192]

---

[190] *Control*, 66.
[191] *Homecoming*, 38.
[192] *Trickster*, 196.

The indoctrination into Catholicism in the residential school further accelerates the intended deconstruction of the brothers' Aboriginal identity.

Told from Gabriel's perspective, the narrator inducts the reader into "the misalignments of the abusive brand of the European Christian mission."[193] Hogeterp-Koopman emphasises that the author ironically names Jeremiah's brother after one of God's messengers.[194] The author reveals the shortcomings of the Christian mission through the depiction of Gabriel's and "thirty-seven newly bald Cree boys" (71) mimicking an English prayer. The students are forced to "to parrot Latin and English phrases while not yet understanding either language."[195] Ignorant of the meaning of the prayers, "Gabriel rattle[s] off the nonsensical syllables as nimbly as he [can], pretending" (71) to understand the meaning. In Jane Hogeterp-Koopman's terms, the mimicking of a ritual with rich theological significance which they have learned from the European missionaries is so ill-explained that it becomes utter nonsense to the students.[196] In one scene, Gabriel, not yet speaking English, misinterprets the prayer:

> "Hello merry, mutter of cod, play for ussinnees, now anat tee ower of ower beth, aw, men." … But, his knees hurting from the cold, hard linoleum, he [cannot] help but wonder why the prayer include[s] the Cree word "*ussinnees*." What need [does] this mutter of cod have of a pebble? (71)

As Hogeterp-Koopman points out, "this passage indicates that the Native student has upheld his own cultural understandings, interpreting and translating the colonial culture through his own."[197]

Furthermore, in a lesson in Christian religion, Highway illustrates how "Native Canadian characters [misinterpret] European Christian sacraments, stories, and liturgies,"[198] and absorb Christianity through their cultural background. By observing the exemplary paper chart of heaven and hell, Jeremiah is confused and distressed when he realises that heaven seems to contain no Indians. Instead, he spots "dark-skinned people" in hell and feels "relieved that they [are] accounted for on this great chart" (60). The narrator depicts Jeremiah's perception of hell "from his cultural point of view."[199] The boy scrutinises the image of hell and interprets it through his own cultural back-

---

[193] *Trickster*, 196.
[194] Cp. *Trickster*, 196.
[195] McKegney, Sam: "From Trickster Poetics to Transgressive Politics." *Studies in American Indian Literatures*, 17.4 (2005), 93. Hereafter referred to as *Politics*.
[196] Cp. *Trickster*, 196.
[197] *Trickster*, 196.
[198] *Trickster*, 196.
[199] *Trickster*, 196.

ground. He observes on the chart that "Hell ... [is] filled with tunnels, and Champion-Jeremiah ha[s] a great affection for tunnels" (60). The tunnels remind him of "the Wuchusk Oochisk River and its unruly tributaries. Champion-Jeremiah [thinks] of the tunnels he and Gabriel made every winter in the deep snow of Eemanapiteepitat" (60). After his observation, he comes to the conclusion that "hell look[s] more engaging" (60). Champion-Jeremiah hopes "to find an accordion player in at least one cave but, to his great disappointment, there [is] no place for musicians of his ilk in hell" (61). The scene shows that for Jeremiah, "the concepts of heaven and hell, good and bad are arbitrary categories, devoid of meaning," and highlights "the limited value of [the missionaries'] societal laws."[200]

The author shows that the intransparency of Roman Catholic values for other cultures hinders a smooth identification of Indians with Christianity. Highway unveils the gaps and fissures of the Christian mission and demonstrates that the incorrect transmission of values confuses the young Indians and catapults them further into ambiguity. Seen through Jeremiah's eyes, the scene demonstrates the bizarre and nonsensical practice of enforced civilisation and Christianisation. Thus the lesson in Christian religion unveils Bhabha's words that "Between the Western sign and its colonial signification there emerges a map of misreading that embarrasses the righteousness of recordation and its certainty of good government."[201]

3.1.3 Cultural Hybridity

Highway exposes how the white Canadians' attempts to assimilate Canada's First Nations prove to be futile since residential schools render them "unsuited for life in Indian as well as in white Canadian society."[202] The Christian education and artistic training render the Cree boys (entirely unsuited [for] their parents' nature-bound style of life). The brothers feel uprooted at home and displaced in the city. Verena Klein underlines that the values of the Christian education are so different from their own that the brothers (become incapable of relating satisfactorily to their Cree home community and to white Canadian society). With their hybrid identities, neither Indian nor Canadian, they (are ill at ease in both societies). The novel reveals a (two-fold diaspora, both spatial and ideological which force[s] the Indigenous Peoples 'to live a disjoined life,'

---

[200] *Homecoming,* 38-39.
[201] *Theory,* 149.
[202] *Homecoming,* 41. All further references in the text are to this edition.

estranged from their Native roots).

When Jeremiah is fifteen, he moves to the city of Winnipeg, Manitoba, where he attends high school. There he experiences feelings of exclusion and not belonging. Jeremiah's isolation in the city discloses the identity crisis resulting from being divorced from traditional culture "while at the same time refused entry into prosperous white Canada."[203] In the city he encounters the daily humiliation of Indians. Consequently, the city becomes for Jeremiah a site of alienation, transformation and denial.[204] In order to gain greater acceptance among white Canadians, he pretends to be 'white'. Jeremiah tries to suppress his Indian identity, especially since in his high school are no Indians: "they [are] all white; not one [speaks] Cree" (102). Jeremiah's self-estrangement and conscious denial of his Indian roots results from a "desire for the cultural other, for forsaking [his] own culture," which mirrors "the English culture of colonialism."[205] As Coral Ann Howells points out, "faced with the everyday humiliation of Native people, Jeremiah's only desire is to escape into his classical music, denying his Indian identity through intellect and art, transforming himself 'into a perfect little 'transplanted European'—anything to survive' (124)."[206]

Jeremiah's rigorous efforts of assimilation and acculturation place him on a self-defeating course of self-denial.[207] Jeremiah suppresses his Indian identity and locks up emotionally. Jeremiah's history lessons in high school are depicted as "a means of denying the past."[208] Jeremiah denies the history of his people. Philip Tew notes that "denying the past is to refuse to recognize its integrity."[209] For Jeremiah's "first theatrical production" (148) at school he "practise[s] his English-Canadian accent ... until his tongue hurt[s]" (146). Moreover, he is ashamed of "his backwoods ungainliness" in "a room filled with white people" (146). The repression of his Nativeness and his mimicry of white Canadians shows his desire for the oppressive culture on the one hand, and the disavowal of his own culture on the other. In the two lonely years in the city he effectively denies his Cree identity and "give[s] up his native tongue to the roar of traffic" (113). When he is finally joined by Gabriel, he has accomplished his linguistic adapta-

---

[203] *Politics*, 80.

[204] Cp. Bak, Hans: "The City as a Site of Trauma and Transformation: Sherman Alexie's 'Indian Killer' and Tomson Highway's 'Kiss of the Fur Queen'." *Anglophonia: French Journal of English Studies*, 25 (2009), 403. Hereafter referred to as *City*.

[205] Wachinger, Tobias A.: *Posing In-Between: Postcolonial Englishness and the Commodification of Hybridity*. Frankfurt am Main: Lang 2003, 144. Hereafter referred to as *In-Between*.

[206] *Queen*, 89.

[207] Cp. *City*, 401.

[208] Tew, Philip: *Contemporary British Novel*. London: Continuum 2004, 182. Hereafter referred to as *British*.

[209] *British*, 182.

tion; his "English [rings] out like a white boy's" (160).

Reunited with his brother Gabriel in Winnipeg, Jeremiah wonders at Gabriel's quick transformation into a city boy. Tobias A. Wachinger argues that the city provides "the ideal breeding ground for multicultural diversity."[210] This ideal breeding ground prompts the boys' quintessential hybridity. Wachinger points out that in the city "all fixed identities are seen as likely to be dissolved and rearranged as in a transnational community."[211] After Gabriel's vacation at home, the brothers "plunge into the city's mecca of consumerism"[212]—Winnipeg's "Polo Park Shopping Mall" (115). Gabriel's transformation from an Indian village boy into a city boy is immense. He literally strips off his Indian appearance and puts on a white boy's city costume. The narrator describes the transformation:

At every store, Gabriel virtually dance[s] into each article of clothing and [stands] before the mirror not so much preening as plotting "his Winnipeg years." Like moulted skin, his old wardrobe accumulated in his multicoloured shopping bags. (119)

The narrator emphasises that Gabriel's "appearance ha[s] changed so dramatically that if Jeremiah had not witnessed the metamorphosis, he would have taken his sibling for a rock star with a tan" (119). He explicitly hints at Gabriel's intermingling of the two antagonistic cultures comprised in his quintessential hybridity: "Gabriel's navy blue windbreaker, his red plaid flannel shirt, his entire person sparked off microscopic waves of campfire smoke, of green spruce boughs, of dew-laden reindeer moss" (114).

In spite of his cultural adaptation, Gabriel does not feel at home in Winnipeg. Gabriel realises his dislocation: "We don't belong here, [...] wanting desperately to burst into tears" (127). On the one hand, like Jeremiah, Gabriel feels lonely and isolated in the city: "What [is] there for a person like him—no friend, not one acquaintance, save Jeremiah, who [does] nothing but play the piano" (126). On the other hand, however, Gabriel's desire for home clashes with the seduction of the manifold possibilities of city life. Inside the mall, Gabriel is stunned by its dimensions and "such an array of wordly wealth, a paradise on earth" (115). Howells underlines that "the two brown Indian[s']" (114)

sense of 'unbelonging' in Winnipeg and their desire for home is in permanent conflict with the excitements induced by the white world of high culture which paradoxically obliterates their identities while offering enormous rewards in a 'newfound language' (153).[213]

---

[210] *In-between*, 157.
[211] *In-between*, 157.
[212] *Politics*, 91.
[213] *Queen*, 89.

The novel shows that the Okimasis brothers occupy an intermediate position equivalent of "Bhabha's theory of third space."[214] According to Bhabha, a colonial hybrid identity always occupies an ambivalent position of in-betweenness. He terms the space in-between in his *The Location of Culture* (1994), 'the third space.'[215] The new cultural hybrid emerges from the cultural clash between the rulers and the ruled. Michel Serres equivalently refers to the man occupying the intermediate position as the "third man."[216] Serres highlights the "vectorial forces of a third element which emerges whenever two subjects enter into a dialogical relationship."[217] The argument of the "third man" who occupies the "third space" goes beyond the essentialist perspective on identity.

On a visit at home, Jeremiah refuses to help his father with fishing and the piling of crates. In order to be able to play the piano, Jeremiah has to be careful with his fingers. Gabriel explains Jeremiah's odd behaviour, "'He doesn't do heavy work, Dad,' […] 'it's bad for his hands'" (193). Their father is disappointed by the notable alien-ation of his children: "visit by visit, word by word, these sons [are] splintering from their subarctic roots, their Cree beginnings" (193). Jeremiah cannot imagine himself returning to his native village and getting a "work at the store" (189). The long absence, evident in the "two-fold diaspora, both spatial and ideological," forces the brothers "'to live a disjoined life,' estranged from their Native roots."[218]

The author's cultural hybridity is not only mirrored in the hybrid identities of his protagonists, but also emerges in the novel's structure. The novel's structure, infused with both the Western literary model and indigenous ways of telling stories, testifies to the author's cultural hybridity. Highway integrates indigenous oral narrative modes in the novel. With its visions, flashbacks and mythological framework, the novel is itself a pioneering instance of the cultural clash. The intermingling of cultures in a literary form is also mirrored in the plot of the novel. The Cree brothers intermix the narrative legacy of the antagonistic cultures in the script of a play. The play *Ulysses Thunderchild* demonstrates Jeremiah's hybridity, for he implements therein features of cultural authority and native authenticity. The creative playwright gives the play a "modern

---

[214] Ikas, Karin, Gerhard Wagner (ed.): "Communicating in the Third Space." *Transnational Literature*, 3.1
(2010).<http://dspace.flinders.edu.au/jspui/bitstream/2328/15136/1/Communicating%20in%20the%20third%20space.pdf> (17.6.2012). Hereafter referred to as *Space*.
[215] Cp. *Space*.
[216] Papastergiadis, Nikos: The Turbulence of Migration: Globalization, Deterritorialization and Hybridity. Oxford: Polity Press 2007, 187. Hereafter referred to as *Migration*.
[217] *Migration*, 187.
[218] *Homecoming*, 35.

twist" (277) by adapting the indigenous Son of Ayash myth to *Ulysses*. The playwright announces that the play will be the "Closest thing the Cree have to their own Ulysses" (277). Jeremiah expounds, "if James Joyce can do 'one day in the life of an Irishman in Dublin, 1903,' why can't I do 'one day in the life of a Cree man in Toronto, 1984'?" (277).

But for all that, for Gabriel the play seems to be "unplayable" (279) because it does not have enough "sounds of native voices, … howling of the north wind, and … figures of Cree mythology."[219] Acknowledging his brother's critique, Jeremiah enhances the play's rootedness in Cree mythology and works (through and beyond the European literary model, transforming it with drum music and dance). After Jeremiah puts the finishing touches on the play's script, the "magic" (280) of the Aboriginal Son of Ayash myth finally works and the play becomes a (smash hit).

3.1.4 The Problem of Translation

One of the building blocks of hybrid identity is the issue of translation. The act of translation constitutes an essential element of hybrid identity, for "the hybrid is formed out of the dual process of displacement and correspondence in the act of translation."[220] As "most of the post-colonial theorists believe […] translation is a matter of culture to be conveyed."[221] They believe that many cultural aspects cannot be easily and understandably conveyed and therefore are not transferable.[222] Gayatri Spivak argues in *Can the Subaltern Speak* (1988) that cultural translation is almost impossible. The problem of translation escalates when one culture and language is more or less powerful, as in the case of colonisation.[223] The limitations of cultural translation, as Spivak contends, can be found in the failings of the mythological and conceptual translations from Cree into English or vice versa. The Cree myth of the Weetigo and Weesageechak shows the limits of cultural translation. Jeremiah says, "you could never get away with a story like that in English" (118). These limits pose a hindrance to intercultural communication.

On the other end of the problematic issue of translation, between the centre and the periphery, the brothers desperately attempt to translate English into Cree. Jeremiah

---

[219] *Queen*, 91. All further references in the text are to this edition.
[220] *Migration*, 194.
[221] Ghadi, Alirza Sadegh: *Cultural Translation And Post Colonialism*.
    <http://www.articlesnatch.com/Article/Cultural-Translation-And-Post-Colonialism/513892#ixzz1RWDQL6lw> (03.05.2012). Hereafter referred to as *Translation*.
[222] Cp. *Translation*.
[223] Cp. *Translation*.

angrily wonders, "How, for God's sake, did one say 'concert pianist' in Cree?" (189). Desperately seeking for corresponding words in Cree, Jeremiah must acknowledge his defeat to Spivak's "violence of silence."[224] Benjamin observes that (no translation can find exact correspondences between different languages). The hybrid, therefore, is formed out of the (awareness of the untranslatable bits that linger on in translation). Faced with the problem of translation, the Cree brothers must painfully acknowledge that "meaning seldom moves across borders with pristine integrity."[225] When Jeremiah asks, "How do you say 'university'? In Cree?" (191), Gabriel realises that "every translation requires a degree of improvisation."[226] He replies, "*Semen*-airy," the closest word Gabriel can get "in his native tongue" (191). Here, the act of translation distorts meaning rather than give it an equivalent translation. The Okimasis brothers sadly learn that accurate translation as a "chasm as unbridgeable as hell separates Cree from English" (190).

Later in the novel, the deadly sick Gabriel reiterates the issue of untranslatability. He fails to find a Cree analogy for AIDS. Contemplating how to tell his mother about his deadly disease, Gabriel says to Jeremiah, "How do you say AIDS in Cree, huh? Tell me, what's the word for HIV?" (296). The illustrated problem of translation between the oppressing and oppressed cultures creates a tension in the cultural hybrids' 'third space,' emergent in "the interstitial and liminal moments of articulation."[227] With its deficiencies, the act of translation buttresses the in-betweenness of hybrid identity.

With his narrative example, Highway substantiates the challenge to the essential-ist models of identity, showing that postcolonial identity is always in a process of construction, negotiation and reshaping. With the novel he demonstrates that "postcolo-nial Native identity is beset with ambivalence" and is filled "with doubles and split selves."[228] Highway's depiction of Jeremiah's identity construction resonates with Hall's argument that identity cannot be seen as originary and self-contained but always contains aspects of emergent and multiple selves.[229] Among the leading postcolonial theorists, Hall, Bhabha and Spivak, there seems to be a general "consensus over the utility of hybridity as an antidote to essentialist subjectivity."[230] Bhabha stresses that (identity is never fixed once and for all, it never coheres into an absolute form). Accord-

---

[224] *Migration*, 192. All further references in the text are to this edition.
[225] *Migration*, 194.
[226] *Migration*, 194.
[227] *Migration*, 194.
[228] *Queen*, 85.
[229] Cp. *Memory*, 8.
[230] *Migration*, 189. All further references in the text are to this edition.

ing to Bhabha, (identity always presupposes a sense of location and a relationship with others). Hybrid identity, however, is preconditioned by displacement, loss and alienation. Hybridity in itself is an unstable concept which entails social transformation. Following Hall, hybrid identity, produced from the exchange between different peripheries, is always incomplete and hence representational of the anti-essentialist perspective on identity.[231]

3.1.5 Impersonation and Restoration

The Cree boys' artistic dedication, Jeremiah a piano artist and Gabriel a ballet dancer, is an effort "to eke out new lives and identities in an Anglophone-Canadian urban ambience."[232] In the Anderson High School production of *The Gondoliers*, Gabriel plays the role of the gondoliers-cum-prince, Giuseppe Palmieri. He is very proud of his capability to perform an Italian faithfully. When he takes his "mask" off, he sees "the other Gabriel" in the mirror (158). Confronted with his Cree identity at the site of his reflection, he sneaks "the Cree out like a sin" (159). The school production mirrors the symbolic performance of the brothers' "new Christianized identities."[233] Gabriel represents Fanon's 'white-masked black,' who cannot strip off the blackness of his skin. The unbridgeable gap between the brothers' masks and their skin colour engenders their traumatic condition.

Highway illustrates that there is no use in pretending what the brothers are not. Their successful performance does not make the brothers happy: "In the mirror, the brothers' mouths smile[…] but their eyes well[…] up with an inexpressible loneliness" (159). On the contrary, the audience finds it "curious, even thought-provoking" to see the "Indian pianist," and "they ha[ve] never imagined" seeing an "Indian-Italian gondolier" (157). Sadly, the fact that the tickets for the brothers' five performances are entirely sold out is predicated upon the brothers' difference rather than their artistic talent. Their hybrid identities, neither Indian nor Anglo-Canadian, are torn between transformation and denial, on the ever-continuing quest for themselves.

While Jeremiah pursues his course of denying his Cree identity, Gabriel reverts to his Indian roots earlier in the novel. He realises the hypocrisy of the Roman Catholic Church and begins to abominate its religion. His multiple sexual abuse by Father

---

[231] Cp. *Migration*, 190.
[232] *City*, 401.
[233] *City*, 401.

Lafleur makes him realise the perversity of Christian religion and he assesses that his ancestors' pagan religion holds more virtue and authenticity. Furthermore, in the solitude of the city, Gabriel has enough time to ponder the injustices done to his family by the Catholic Church. He remembers how, imposed by the priest when he was five years old, his father "stopped speaking to his sister" (129) for leaving her violent husband. Thereupon his mother "and her children were forced to communicate with her by subterfuge" (129). Consequently, he realises the Catholic Church's supremacy in the process of splitting of his family and sides with his Cree identity.

However, the turning point for Jeremiah's negation of his Cree identity is initiated when "Amanda Clear Sky, dusky Indian maiden of eighteen years" (148), appears in his class. She is the only other Indian student "in the school filled with two thousand white middle-class kids" (149). Her appearance plays a crucial role for Jeremiah's reorientation. Amanda functions as a cultural leader for Jeremiah. The Indian girl confronts him with his Cree identity and deliberately evokes his memories of Indian culture and history. She reminds Jeremiah: "You just shouldn't forget that we have a history, too, that's all," and figuratively tears off his Christian mask: "What use is there pretending to be what you are not?" (149). She asks him, where is "your *noble* Cree heritage?" (172). Subsequently, Amanda invites him to The Winnipeg Indian Friendship Centre (162), where Jeremiah walks in and by chance meets her and her grandmother. However, he finds the whole Indian performance ridiculous and feels ashamed of the people who attempt "to revive dead customs in the middle of a city" (172). Feeling awkward and misplaced, he leaves the place "mumbl[ing] some excuse" (176).

Later, the Okimasis brothers have a religious argument, where "Gabriel's confidence, like his Cree, [blooms]" (183). Whereas Gabriel reverts to his Cree roots, his brother stubbornly pursues his course of self-denial and insists that "there's no such thing" as "Indian religion" (183). Gabriel counters him with the hypocrisy of Catholicism: "Where do you think them priests get their jollies?" (184). Gabriel utters his dissatisfaction with Christianity, claiming that his knowledge of it "make[s] one lose respect for organized religion" (183). Their argument over their Cree identity escalates into a fight: "With his last drop of rage, Jeremiah pull[s] Gabriel's neck to a breaking point" (208). In his rage, Gabriel accuses his brother of solidarity with their Catholic oppressors: "How can you still listen to their sick propaganda? After what they did to us?" (208). He is disgusted at Jeremiah's attempts to disguise himself and his stubborn efforts "to become a whiteman" (207).

The turning point finally comes when Jeremiah, now twenty, is the first Indian to win the Crookshank Memorial Trophy for his brilliant piano concert. While Gabriel is in Toronto, after their argument about his homosexual relationship with Gregory, Jeremiah feels lonely and misses his brother. Suddenly he realises that his brother was right that he cannot escape being Indian, that he cannot flee from himself, cannot be 'white'. At this point he finally reverts back to his Cree roots. In the moment of self-realisation he thinks about the unbridgeable chasm of his Christianised identity:

> He ha[s] tried. Tried to change the meaning of his past, the roots of his hair, the colour of his skin, but he [is] one of them. What [is] he to do with Chopin? Open a conservatory on Eemanapiteepitat hill? Whip its residents into Cree Philharmonic Orchestra? (215)

From that moment begins Jeremiah's path of self-reconstruction. Devastated by his disorientation, he begins to drink. He gives up his career as a concert pianist and instead picks up drunks off the streets. He works as a social worker in the "Winnipeg Indian Friendship Centre, Street Patrol" (221). With all the violence, abuse and mistreatment of Indians in the city, Jeremiah wonders after six years, "how much longer could he endure this [...] purgatory [of] his people?" (221).

Later, on his father's deathbed, Jeremiah finds encouragement and confirmation for the decolonisation of his mind. The juxtaposition of the Christian and the Indigenous, also emblematic of his sons' hybrid identities, is illustrated on Abraham's deathbed, "the Cree descant whirring, light as foam, over the [priest's] English dirge" (227).[234] Jeremiah's witnessing of "the battle between competing spiritual systems"[235] on his father's deathbed "becomes an essential component" within his life for "his ultimate self-definition."[236] His father's Cree legacy secures Jeremiah's intention to restore his suppressed Native identity.

After Abraham's death, Jeremiah assumes a new daytime job, in the Muskoosis Club, where he writes and teaches Indian children about their cultural heritage. The job offers him "the potential for personal and cultural growth on Native terms."[237] There, he finds a (vocabulary for the articulation of selfhood [and] determines the identity he will claim). By recounting to (a younger generation its inheritance of cultural stories), he chooses (an identity characterised by creativity, not violence). The job fosters the

---

[234] Cp. *Politics*, 94.
[235] *Control*, 70.
[236] *Control*, 70.
[237] *Politics*, 101. All further references in the text are to this edition.

reconstruction of his Indian identity.

When Gabriel dies of AIDS, Jeremiah supports his brother's wish for a traditional cleansing ceremony. Against their mother's earnest wish for the Catholic absolution, Jeremiah engages Amanda's grandmother, a Cree medicine woman for the last traditional ritual for his dying brother. Defending the ceremony, Jeremiah cries: "We're Indians! We have a right to conduct our own religious ceremonies, just like everyone else!" (305).

The Cree brothers' process of identity construction foregrounds displacement, loss and alienation. The process of mixing and engaging with white Canadian society generates the hybridisation of the brothers' cultural identities. Jeremiah's "shifting self symbolizes [such] a hybridization of identity."[238] Marked by (acculturation), which is (the process of absorption of one culture by another), the brothers suffer from alienation in both societies. The shifting selves stand in a permanent conflict with each other and engender a sense of cultural incongruence and confusion. Highway reveals that the protagonist's (predicament of cultural 'inbetweenness') with (a wider series of transformations) is a legacy of (socially unjust practices) of the colonial condition.

The novel shows how colonial cultural hybridity is intrinsically traumatising to the consciousness of the colonised self. The condition of oppression and marginalisation induces confusion, ruptures and gaps in the construction of the self. The novel exposes that the multiple self of the cultural hybrid is subjected to a series of traumatising events as a consequence of the colonial condition.

3.2 Trauma, Mythology and Communication

Tomson Highway's *Kiss of the Fur Queen* is a highly mythological trauma novel. In his trauma novel, the author delineates the impact of his childhood trauma of spatial and ideological diaspora with the ensuing insidious consequences for his and his younger brother's lives. The tragic narrative about the brothers' forced relocation which deprived them of their parental home and love, their language, their spiritual beliefs and cultural traditions, invokes "the atrocities suffered by the Aboriginal Peoples in Canada."[239] Highway enriches the post-colonial trauma discourse with significant information about Aboriginal means for dealing with trauma. The novelist explores the trauma of his past with the help of Aboriginal Cree mythology. Moreover, he discloses the significance of

---

[238] *British*, 159. All further references in the text are to this edition.
[239] *Homecoming*, 35.

Aboriginal ethics in dealing with trauma. With his foray into post-colonial trauma discourse, the author reinforces the argument that Western trauma theory is not cross-culturally applicable.

3.2.1 The Trauma of Abuse

The trauma of the Okimasis brothers' early uprooting is immensely aggravated by their sexual abuse at the residential school. Both brothers are frequently abused by the priests of the boarding school. The abuse "will indelibly inscribe itself into the lives of both protagonists"[240] and will determine their sexual orientation as adults. Jeremiah's sexual abuse promotes his abusive sexuality and his inability to establish relationships with women: "He couldn't get erect. His sex was dead" (260). Gabriel's sexual abuse triggers his masochistic homosexuality. As Mark Shackleton claims, "Gabriel's promiscuous homosexuality," leading to AIDS, "a product of his sexual initiation by Lafleur," is "symptomatic on the individual level of the effect of the Christian Church on the lives of Aboriginals worldwide."[241]

The Okimasis brothers' sexual abuse comes on top of their loss of home and family. In order to escape the pain of loss, Jeremiah returns to his (childhood place of happiness ... in his dreams at residential school). But his (dreams are brutally shattered by the sexually abusive Principal of the school). The narrator illustrates the scene of the abuse of the eight-year-old Jeremiah: "Father Roland Lafleur, oblate of Mary Immaculate, unbutton[s] his cassock, unzipped[s] his trousers. So white, [thinks] Champion-Jeremiah, so big." He portrays the carrying out of the crime: "the holy man inside him, lining of his rectum being torn, the pumping and pumping and pumping" (287). Jeremiah, deprived of his Cree identity, is now at the mercy of the Catholic perpetrator, "His hair [is] gone; he ha[s] no power" (74). He feels also powerless to fulfil his responsibility as elder sibling; he cannot spare Gabriel from the same horrific experience.

The novel's central crisis involves the rape of Gabriel by the principal of Birch Lake Residential School, Father Roland Lafleur. Though the assault on Gabriel is told indirectly, due to the figurative language "the audience is never left with any doubt that

---

[240] *Politics*, 87.
[241] Shackleton, Mark: "The Return of the Native American: The Theme of Homecoming in Contemporary Native North American Fiction." *The Atlantic Literary Review*, 3.2 (2002), 160-61. Hereafter referred to as *Return*. All further references in the text are to this edition.

the abuse has occurred."[242] Sam McKegney notes that the boys' trauma, "the horrible act of abuse [...] is told from the perspective of both brothers."[243]

Highway depicts Jeremiah's process of repression and dissociation as he witnesses the traumatic event. At the peak of the narrative's crises, the sexual abuse of young Gabriel by Lafleur, Jeremiah resorts to Cree mythology in order to comprehend the otherwise incomprehensible event. Told from Jeremiah's perspective, Father Lafleur's molestation of Gabriel is depicted in Cree spiritual terms. He compares the principal of the school to "the Weetigo feasting on human flesh" (79). The Weetigo is "in traditional Cree theology and orature the most terrifying of creatures [...]; referred to by some as a cannibalistic human, by others as a monster or spirit," and its "defining characteristic is its consumption of human flesh."[244] Moreover, "Weetigos have an insatiable hunger and an ability to turn other humans into Weetigos."[245] As McKegney argues, "Highway overtly likens the sexual assault on Gabriel to an attack by the cannibal spirit Weetigo, identifying the perpetrator, in Cree spiritual terms, as the most heinous of monsters."[246] Jeremiah's configuration of the horrible event in Cree spiritual terms is a characteristic account of dissociation, a protective mechanism of the brain evolved to cope with the terrifying event.

The moment of Jeremiah's experience of Gabriel's abuse resonates a protective manoeuvre of the brain: "Jeremiah open[s] his mouth and move[s] his tongue, but his throat [goes] dry. No sound [comes] except a ringing in his ears" (80). Jeremiah's brain immediately represses his traumatic experience: "But some chamber deep inside his mind slammed permanently shut. ... He ha[s] not seen what he was seeing" (80). Jeremiah represses the traumatising experience.

Victims of rape or child abuse often respond to abuse in terms of posttraumatic stress disorder (PTSD).[247] As Laura Di Prete explains, the symbols and metaphors of Cree legends "mimic psychic dynamics of repression and dissociation, which rise to protect the mind from an experience too intense and devastating to be accommodated from within."[248] Dissociation is correlated with acute trauma reactions and emerges as a

---

[242] *Politics*, 89.

[243] *Politics*, 87.

[244] *Control*, 70.

[245] Fagan, Kristina: Weesageechak Meets the Weetigo: Storytelling, Humour, and Trauma in the Fiction of Richard Van Camp, Tomson Highway, and Eden Robinson. *Studies in Canadian Literature*, 34.1 (2009), 217. Hereafter referred to as *Weesageechak*.

[246] *Control*, 70.

[247] Cp. *Unclaimed*, 11.

[248] Di Prete, Laura: *Foreign Bodies: Trauma, Corporeality and Textuality in Contemporary American Culture*. New York: Routledge 2006, 5. Hereafter referred to as *Bodies*.

defensive coping strategy to protect the traumatised.[249] The "dissociative manoeuvres" of the brain provide an immediate relief "in the face of overwhelming horror and traumatic stress."[250] Furthermore, dissociation is linked to later development of PTSD and other pathology.[251]

In stark contrast to his brother, the victim of the molestation perceives the dramatic affront to his sexuality in Christian symbolic terms. When Father Lafleur bends over Gabriel with his crucifix dangling from his neck, Gabriel perceives "the subtly throbbing motion of the priest's upper body" that makes "the naked Jesus Christ [...] rub his body against [his] lips" (78). The narrator depicts Gabriel's perception of his abuse: "The pleasure in his centre welled so deep that he was about to open his mouth and swallow whole the living flesh [...] this man nailed to the cross was a living, breathing man, tasting like Gabriel's most favourite food, warm honey" (79). Gabriel's perception of the rape in Christian terminology will direct his self-destructive path embroiled in masochistic homosexuality, leading to his eventual death from AIDS.

3.2.2 The Trauma of Civilisation

The author illustrates the hopeless situation for Indians living in Canada's urban areas. When Jeremiah moves to the city of Winnipeg he suffers from solitude and isolation. As Hans Bak rightfully contends, the city becomes for Jeremiah a site of trauma and loss.[252] In his desperation, solitary "in the midst of half a million people" (104), "at times near tears," Jeremiah even thinks "to drown himself" (170). In the Winnipeg Central Library, Jeremiah finds a shelter to protect himself from "the suicide-inducing loneliness of city Saturdays" (170). With no place to go to and no one to talk to, he feels extremely lonely and excluded. The only activity available to him to bridge the lonely nights in Winnipeg is playing piano in his "basement room on the north side of the city" (103). Jeremiah's "avoidance behaviour"—his "withdraw[al] into a protective shelter of isolation"[253]—resonates as a symptom of PTSD. In his despair, Jeremiah seeks consolation in "his father's lessons on solitude: how time alone could be spent without need for crying," but suddenly he discovers that he "never told [him] how to spend time alone in

---

[249] Cp. *Cognitive*, 642.
[250] *Cognitive*, 642.
[251] Cp. *Cognitive*, 642.

[252] Cp. *City* , 403.
[253] *Cognitive*, 626.

the midst of half a million people," where "stars don't shine at night, trees don't speak" (103–4).

Moreover, on the streets of Winnipeg he experiences the brutality of racism, violence and the humiliation of Indian women. He even becomes a witness of crime as he recognises an Indian woman in a newspaper. He saw her as she got into a car before she was killed. He reads in "the Winnipeg *Tribute*: the naked body of Evelyn Rose McCrae—long-lost daughter of Mistik Lake—had been found in a ditch on the city's outskirts, a shattered beer bottle lying gently, like a rose, deep inside her crimson-soaked sex" (107). When he wants to report the important information to the Winnipeg police, he is confronted with racism himself. The police "paid little heed to the observations of fifteen-year-old Indian boys" (107). Consequently, his distress escalates and he begins ceaselessly to play "the piano until his fingers bl[e]ed" (107).

In school, Gabriel experiences another humiliating experience related to Christianity. When the brothers play Jesus in the residential school, Gabriel impersonates Jesus. He is nailed to the cross by Jeremiah and other children. When it is time for supper, the boy is left "hanging [on his own] in the gathering gloom," and is forced to free himself from the "binding ropes" (86). When he finally arrives for supper, the children turn him into ridicule because he still wears "his spruce-root crown of thorns" (87). The explosive laughter of the children and their "pointing fingers worse than nails" consolidate "his vow of vengeance" (87) on his brother. The incident strains the brothers' relationship and triggers a conflict which will later assume a dramatic shape.

3.2.3 The Communication of Trauma

The narrator of the novel never makes direct or angry accusations, nor does he mention any of the traumatising events directly. Instead, Highway elaborates the Cree brothers' trauma with the help of Aboriginal ethics of storytelling. The indirect discourse employed by the narrator is "a common Aboriginal American speech phenomenon in which the speaker avoids directly stating something to the listener or listeners, instead implying meaning and expecting those hearing to make meaning for themselves."[254] The Aboriginal ethic has (a strong cultural prohibition) against expressing (anger and grief, especially towards family members). For the reason that in Aboriginal societies

---

[254] *Weesageechak*, 207. All further references in the text are to this edition.

communal harmony is regarded as superior to individual well-being, it is seen as (ethically wrong" to bear witness "if it is destructive to community harmony).

In strong contrast to Aboriginal ethic, Western psychologists encourage direct communication of trauma. They insist on it as a healthy strategy for coping with traumatic experience. As Vickroy points out, "trauma researchers have emphasised— that for healing to take place, survivors must find ways to tell their stories and to receive some social acknowledgment if not acceptance."[255] They insist that "bearing witness is essential for individual and group survival of trauma."[256] The direct communication of trauma "violates the traditional ethics of Northern Aboriginal peoples" and "indirect discourse" in the context of trauma "is not always recognised within Western communi- cative practices."[257] In *Worlds of Hurt* (1996) Kali Tal disapproves of the alleviating capacity of bearing witness and describes it as an "aggressive, angry [and] individualist" act.[258] Testimonial writing about trauma alone can be harmful to the soul of the victim and even increase the suffering. It must be underlined that "white Western notions of justice and psychological health" are "culturally formed and informed," and therefore constitute "the antitheses of the traditional ethical principles of many Aboriginal peoples."[259]

The brothers' reluctance to tell their parents about what is happening to them in school resonates with the Aboriginal ethic. The brothers cannot tell their parents what Father Lafleur does to them in school. They do not want to disturb the harmony of their family and believe that their parents will not believe them anyway. Abraham and Mariesis Okimasis are devoted Catholics and firmly believe in the benevolence of the Catholic Church. They believe that the priests do the best for their children and save them and their Cree community from sorrow and banishment. In this context, "not speaking" about the traumatic event becomes "the preferred response to an uncomfort- able situation."[260] They escape the distressing and confusing conversation with their parents: "Jeremiah was absolutely sure Gabriel's silence would remain until the day they died" (92).

Similarly, the parents also show reluctance when it comes to speaking about his- torical traumas in the presence of their children. They adhere to the cultural prohibition

---

[255] *Survival*, 19.
[256] *Survival*, 19.
[257] *Weesageechak*, 207-8.
[258] Tal, Kali: *Worlds of Hurt: Reading the Literatures of Trauma.* Cambridge: Cambridge University Press 1996, 7. Hereafter referred to as *Hurt*.
[259] *Weesageechak*, 208.
[260] *Weesageechak*, 209.

against expressing anger and sorrow. When the brothers inquire about a ghost fire they see on an island where a shaman had once been captured by the Catholic Church, their mother's only response is "Don't look at it" (90).[261]

However, despite the cultural prohibition, the brothers feel the need to talk about the abuse. The ethic of communal welfare thus additionally burdens their plight and inhibits their wish to tell their parents the truth about the abuse. The ambivalence of their situation forces them to evolve alternative ways for coping with the trauma of their abuse. Highway presents alternative methods to solve the dilemma of not speaking. The Cree brothers employ their artistic vocations to express themselves through dance and music. Gabriel becomes a talented ballet dancer and Jeremiah a highly talented classical piano player. Highway employs his artistic endowment to construe a testimony based on the Cree way of telling stories and making myths. His artistic vocation, strengthened with the mythical weaponry of the Cree mythology, provides him with an uninvestigated method of self-therapy within Western trauma theory.

3.2.4 The Accommodation of Trauma

The novel exposes the indigenous means for accommodating and dealing with trauma through myths, legends and humour. In dealing with their trauma the Cree boys "explicitly link their trauma to the realms of dreams, relating their memories to 'bad dream power'."[262] Gabriel asks Jeremiah in the presence of their parents,

> "Do 'machipoowamoowin' [bad dream power] mean what Father Lafleur do to the boys at school?" Although he wanted to tickle his brother with his light-hearted joke, Gabriel's question ended with an eerie, spectral chuckle that could have popped out of a bubble of his blood. (91)

The memory of their abuse is rendered humorous. Kristina Fagan points out that (it is not surprising that the boys find something funny in their abuse). She continues, (for them, residential school was an absurd mix of Catholicism and sexuality, of caretaking and abuse, of celibacy and sado-masochism). Humour relieves the dilemma of silence and is a means of indirect communication. Humour is also (one way of expressing [the] incongruity) experienced by the boys at the hands of the priests. The scene of Gabriel's communion is also full of humour and absurdity. Gabriel laughs openly at the hypocrisy

---

[261] Cp. *Weesageechak*, 215.

[262] *Weesageechak*, 216. All further references in the text are to this edition.

of the priest who gives him communion:

> The Jesuit's crotch was arrestingly level with Gabriel's line of vision [...] Gabriel's gaze raked its way up the belly, chest, and neck to the face, where he knew he had induced a flashing spasm in the holy man's gaze. The Cree youth [...] watched with glee as celibacy-by-law drove mortal flesh to the brink [...] a laugh exploded where his "Amen" should have been. The laugh was so loud—the joke so ludicrous, the sham so extreme [...] (180-81)

The author illustrates how the brothers investigate their trauma through Indian mythology. The boys recall the traditional Cree story of the Weetigo and Weesageechak, the Cree trickster, during their shopping visit to the mall in Winnipeg. The narrator compares the brothers' entry into the mall to the Weesageechak's entry into the Weetigo's bumhole. In the mall, the brothers call to mind the traditional orature: Weesageechak, "disguised as a weasel, [...] crawls up the Weetigo's bumhole" (118) and "chew[s] the Weetigo's entrails [...] from the inside out" (120) "in order to kill the horrible monster," and the Weasel "comes back out with his white fur coat covered with shit" (118). Moreover, throughout the novel, Highway associates the Weetigo with sexual abusers: "a monster who eats little boys" (271).[263]

During their shopping tour in the mall, Gabriel enters the men's washroom and is confronted by a man exposing himself, "holding in his hand a stalk of fireweed so pink, so mauve that Gabriel could not help but look" (120). Through the metaphorical language of Cree storytelling, the narrator circumvents direct communication. Due to Gabriel's history of repetitive sexual abuse by the priests, he has evolved a masochistic inclination towards homophile desire. The experience of eroticised desire at the sight of the man's nude genitalia brings back Gabriel's childhood trauma. The encounter illustrates the repetitive pattern of trauma which materialises when a person is exposed to traumatic stressors, and which haunts the victim throughout his or her entire life. The image of the man's genitalia shifts "the Cree Adonis" back to the scene of the crime: he "[can] taste, upon the buds that line [...] his tongue, warm honey" (121).

After the sinister encounter, Gabriel continues the story of the weasel and the Weetigo: "'My coat!'" moaned the weasel. 'My nice coat is covered with shit!'" Gabriel connects the mythical story to "the image of a certain man aflame with fireweed clinging to his senses with pleasurable insistence" (121) as Jeremiah continues: "Feeling sorry for the hapless trickster, God dipped him in the river to clean his coat. But he held

---

[263] Cp. *Weesageechak*, 217.

him by the tail, so its tip stayed dirty" (121). Gabriel completes the story: "And to this day, [...] the weasel's coat is white but for the black tip of the tail" (121). With Gabriel's utterance the narrator implicitly points at the connection between Gabriel's masochistic sexuality and the weasel's stained tip of tail.

However, "the brothers' excursion to the belly of the beast becomes somewhat different than that of the trickster."[264] McKegney points out the difference: "the boys don't enter the mall to destroy it but rather implicate themselves in its process."[265] For "they go there to become more Euro-Canadian."[266] Thus, in a direct reference to the myth, (the white weasel with a black tip of the tail) becomes (the two Cree brothers covered by white cultural costumes, with only the darkness of their faces remaining unmasked). McKegney contends that (the Okimasis brothers are, in effect, shit out by the beast—still very much alive, although soulless—whose characteristics now taint their Cree bodies). At the close of the chapter, Highway draws a comparison between the Cree myth and the consequences of forced civilisation on the Cree brothers: "Grey and soulless, the mall loom[s] behind them, the rear end of a beast that, having gorged itself, expels its detritus" (121).

The brothers' conversation in the Polo Park Shopping Mall in Winnipeg illustrates the brothers' attempts to approach their childhood traumas with the help of Cree mythology. Following Cree mythology, Weesageechak is associated with resistance to abuse.[267] Fagan argues that the brothers deal with their abuse by diving into it, comparably to the weasel diving into the Weetigo.[268] Accordingly, she suggests that "Gabriel is using the traditional story to try to understand his own life, to develop his own 'trauma theory.'"[269] Gabriel takes a self-destructive path to understand his trauma. He does it by "willingly entering into a world of promiscuity and sexual self-abuse that eventually leads to his death."[270] Jeremiah chooses different means of diving into the monster. His means is his immersion in school, classical music and religion.[271]

---

[264] *Politics*, 92.
[265] *Politics*, 92.
[266] *Politics*, 92. All further references in the text are to this edition.
[267] Cp. *Weesageechak*, 217.
[268] Cp. *Weesageechak*, 218.
[269] *Weesageechak*, 218.
[270] *Weesageechak*, 218.
[271] Cp. *Weesageechak*, 218.

3.2.5 In the Shadow of Trauma

The boys' conduct of their lives after the multiple abuse assumes a disturbing pattern. Their behaviour as described in the novel exhibits also other symptoms of PTSD. Granofsky points out that "one of the symptoms of PTSD, 're-experiencing the trau-matic event,' corresponds roughly to the initial miming of trauma characteristic of the trauma novel."[272] As Fagan notes, the Cree boys "also imitate their abusers, both artistically and personally," concluding that their "artistic creation, an adult develop-ment of their childhood skits, are also a way of re-enacting trauma."[273] She contends, "Highway is working within Aboriginal traditions" and expresses the brothers' "painful experience" and memories "through destructive behaviour, through visions and dreams, and through jokes and stories."[274]

The brothers' theatrical productions provide an appropriate way for dealing with trauma since music and dance are excellent means for the implementation of Aboriginal ethics of indirect communication. The brothers integrate Cree mythology into the process of re-enacting their traumas on stage. Jeremiah dives into his abuse on the page and on the stage, like Weesageechak dives into the Weetigo, in an effort to destroy it.[275] As the result of their sexual abuse, the brothers "create imitations of their own abuse" through "self-destructive behaviour" and a tendency towards "the abuse of others."[276] The abusive event of their trauma haunts them through their repetitive destructive actions,[277] symptomatic of PTSD.

Jeremiah's inclination towards the abuse of others is illustrated in a scene wherein a six-year-old Cree boy confesses that he, too, is a victim of abuse. The child responds to Jeremiah's wrapping of sexual abuse in the Cree spiritual terms. After hearing his teacher telling that "A Weetigo is a monster who eats little boys" (271), the little boy hugs Jeremiah. With his "hot faced buried in his groin" he declares, "A Weetigo ate me" (271). McKegney points out that "to Jeremiah's shock and dismay the child then enacts the monster's trademark mastication, biting into his teacher's 'faded blue denim' and causing 'a needle longer than an arm' to shoot up Jeremiah's spine."[278] In the wake of the traumatic flashback of his own abuse, the teacher disentangles himself from the

---

[272] *Novel*, 10.
[273] *Weesageechak*, 218.
[274] *Weesageechak*, 216.
[275] Cp. *Weesageechak*, 219.
[276] *Weesageechak*, 211.
[277] Cp. *Weesageechak*, 210.
[278] *Politics*, 100.

child. However, sexually aroused by the corporeal closeness of the boy, he gets "a raging hard-on" (271).

Highway concludes the chapter with the statement, "For Jeremiah, jail was no-where near enough" (272). As Sam McKegney points out, "although directed at the child's abuser, this line elucidates the precariousness of Jeremiah's own position, in the wake of the return of his own repressed past."[279] After the confrontation with "his latent capacity to become an abuser" himself, Jeremiah must restrain himself in order not to repeat it and "must decide whether he will become the Weetigo"[280] himself or not.

Through the myth of the Weetigo and Weesageechak, Highway provides alternative methods for reading and dealing with trauma. Highway shows that talking about traumatic experience and bearing witness is not necessarily helpful in Aboriginal societies. On the contrary, direct communication of trauma may prove fatal to group harmony of indigenous communities. Putting communal welfare over individual well-being, Aboriginal peoples provide alternative approaches for dealing with trauma. The metaphoric and symbolic representation of trauma through Indian mythology discloses a culturally charged level of coping with trauma. It unveils the metaphorical apparatus of Cree mythology, which provides a tool for self-exploration of individual trauma. Highway shows that through Aboriginal myth trauma can be accessed, explored and appropriated.

On the whole, apart from the above-discussed imprecise classification of the nature of colonial trauma and the respective posttraumatic stress disorder in the context of colonialism, the novel shows other deficiencies of the classical trauma theory. The disclosure of alternative methods for coping and dealing with trauma supports the argument that "Western trauma theory may be insufficient in understanding Aboriginal expressions of trauma."[281] Highway's novel supports the assumption that Western understanding of trauma "cannot illuminate 'non-Western' trauma because it remains locked in a one-dimensional 'event theory' of trauma—what Van Styvendale usefully calls the 'accident model'."[282] With the exposure of the Indian philosophy of trauma the novel calls into question Western ways of communicating and dealing with trauma. Therefore, the novel calls into doubt the cross-cultural applicability of the leading Western trauma theory and implies a "rethinking of trauma as collective, spatial, and

---

[279] *Politics*, 100.
[280] *Control*, 73.
[281] *Weesageechak*, 205.
[282] Rothberg, Michael: "Decolonizing Trauma Studies: A Response." *Studies in the Novel*, 40.1,2 (2008), 228. Hereafter referred to as *Decolonizing*.

material (instead of individual, temporal, and linguistic)," which would break "the hold of a singular model."[283] Thus *Kiss of the Fur Queen* expands Western trauma theories and suggests the need "to include a wider variety of culturally informed systems for understanding the world."[284]

3.3 Resistance, Healing and Reconstruction

Tomson Highway composed his novel after his younger brother René "died of an AIDS-related illness in October 1990."[285] The novel provides a means for the individual healing of the author. After the premature death of his brother, the traumatised playwright and concert pianist experiences the need to explore and accommodate the recent trauma, and the legacy of the post-residential school era. He begins to write his first and only novel, *Kiss of the Fur Queen*, in 1992, and finishes it in 1998. The writing down of the trauma of his past has a therapeutic effect on the author. Through the novel Highway alleviates his pain and comes to terms with his traumas. Moreover, the novelist pursues a political goal with the novel. He works towards the restoration and acknowledgement of Indian culture in white Canada.

According to the psychotherapeutic understanding, the process of writing of one's trauma activates the trauma memory and thus promotes recovery in several ways.[286] One of these ways provides the victim with the feelings of "'safety,' where the individual feels in control or capable of managing his or her surroundings."[287] A commonly investigated method among psychotherapists is the integration of traumatic memory into a narrative form. As they found out, (the victims' ability to turn their story into a coherent narrative appears to be directly related to their recovery). Moreover, they regard (one's ability to sensibly narrate an event [as] necessary for physical and psychological health).

Moreover, apart from "the healing that comes from narrativization"[288] Highway-Jeremiah's process of writing creates "a place wherein the future is nurtured."[289] As a healing process, the "positive reinterpretation of [the] traumatic event, requires [him] to think about whatever positive gains or lessons can be gleaned from the horrific experi-

---

[283] *Decolonizing*, 228.
[284] *Weesageechak*, 219.
[285] *Politics*, 87.
[286] Cp. *Cognitive*, 647.
[287] *Cognitive*, 647. All further references in the text are to this edition.
[288] *Bodies*, 18.
[289] Control, 73.

ence."[290] Through this tactic, the focus lies on the positive effect of reinterpretation and the victim readjusts his experience to the future and thus achieves an alleviation of his painful experiences. As psychotherapists profess, "such positive reinterpretations are therapeutic since they allow the victim to see meaning in the world and to improve their self image, feeling stronger and more capable of confronting adversity."[291] As McKegney properly notes, "Highway identifies the productive path Jeremiah must take, a path with enormous potential for regeneration."[292]

3.3.1 The Power of Cree Mythology

In the novel, Jeremiah returns to the moment of his father's death. This key moment shapes Jeremiah's future as an Indian, for his "spiritual crisis comes after his father's death."[293] During his last absolution, Abraham tells his sons the Son of Ayash myth. According to the traditional Cree orature, the Son of Ayash is "abandoned on an island by an evil father and must endure ordeals before he can 'rejoin... his mother' and fix the wounded world."[294] In "the mythic struggle [...] the heroic Son of Ayash [fights against] the dreaded Weetigo."[295] Abraham relates:

> "My son." [...] "The world has become too evil. With these magic weapons, make a new world," said the mother of the hero, the Son of Ayash [...] So the Son of Ayash took the weapons and, on a magic water snake, journeyed down into the realm of the human soul, where he met [...] Evil after evil [...] the most fearsome among them the man who ate human flesh. (227)

When Abraham says, "The world has become too evil. With these magic weapons, make a new world," his sons witness that "this most Catholic of men" resorts "to pagan tales for the third time that [the brothers can] recall" (227). After his death, the Cree mythology assumes an important significance for Jeremiah. As McKegney points out, "only later in the novel," when Jeremiah becomes himself a writer and begins examining the past, "can he assimilate the tales of the Weetigo and the Son of Ayash into his own life story."[296]

Additionally to the encouragement through his father's words, a vision of the Fur Queen disguised as an Arctic fox appears following his father's death. Howells argues that the apparition of the Arctic fox "marks the beginning of Jeremiah's psychological

---

[290] *Cognitive*, 647.
[291] *Cognitive*, 647.
[292] *Politics*, 101.
[293] *Queen*, 90.
[294] *Control*, 69.
[295] *Control*, 69.
[296] *Control*, 72.

and spiritual healing."[297] The Arctic fox addresses him with the words, "You ain't got much time before that grand finale. So get your little Cree ass out there" (233). Thus inspired by the Son of Ayash myth and the Fur Queen, Jeremiah sets out to combat his trauma and reinvent anew the world the Catholic Church endeavoured to extinguish.

The Cree myth re-emerges during the incident of Jeremiah's crisis with the child. The author explores how Jeremiah's groundbreaking experience with the Indian boy changes his conception of himself and of his trauma. During his time at the Muskoosis Club of Ontario, the centre for Native youth, Jeremiah tells the children the myth he has learned from his father: "Our hero, the Son of Ayah, has to be careful, for he is entering the dark places of the human soul where he will meet evil creatures like … the Weeti-go" (271). At the critical moment with the boy, the Son of Ayash myth enables Jeremiah to identify his own "dark place of the human soul."[298] When the teacher experiences the unwanted arousal, the myth assists his resistance to temptation. As McKegney elucidates, the myth encourages him to wage a battle "within the self" similarly to "the mythic battle between the Son of Ayash and the Weetigo."[299] However, as McKegney notes, he does not fight against an external force, but against one within himself.

After the shocking incident with the child, Jeremiah determines that his daytime job as teacher at The Muskoosis Club of Ontario (269) is insufficient for his personal healing. The incident reveals the destructive power inherent to his own traumatic experience of abuse. Highway reveals how Jeremiah "actively prevents himself from feasting on others like the Weetigo, seeking instead emotional, spiritual, and psycho-logical nourishment in the creative process."[300] Thus after "his crisis with the child," Jeremiah is "harkening back to the initial portrayal of abuse," and is described as "hunched at a typewriter," "like a bear with a honeypot" (273).[301] Instead of passing on his trauma to others and thus continuing the chain reaction of the perpetrator-victim scenario, he circumvents the abusive nature of his trauma by withdrawing into the process of writing. On "the old typewriter," Jeremiah "pick[s] at the letters gingerly," thereby figuratively aggregating the magic weapons he will need for his fight against the dark places of the human soul—"a spear, an axe, a fox's pelt" (275). McKegney points out that

---

[297] *Queen*, 90.
[298] *Control*, 73.
[299] *Control*, 73.
[300] *Politics*, 101.
[301] *Politics*, 101.

like Highway, Jeremiah re-conceptualizes his life in narrative terms of Cree spirituality and traditional orature, made relevant to the contemporary moment through creative adaptation, invention, and augmentation, a process that affords him the creative weaponry to defeat the Weetigo of his past.[302]

Due to his creative weaponry Jeremiah-Champion feels equipped for the defeat of the trauma of his past. The assembly of the myth's magic weaponry proves to be vital for Jeremiah's revision and the process of healing the dark places of his soul. Through the symbolic appropriation of the magic weapons from his father's last tale Jeremiah draws strength to withstand temptation and therefore breaches the cycle of violence.

In the process of their spiritual revival the brothers devote themselves to creative theatrical work. As McKegney points out, quite in the sense of their father, "the brothers ultimately explore in their theatrical work, the creation through art of 'a new world'."[303] During the brothers' performance of a piece by Gabriel, they implement their father's advice. After the successful performance, "Gabriel knew that this magic had worked… Through the brothers, as one, and through a chamber as vast as the north, an old man's voice passed. 'My son,' is sighed, 'with these magic weapons, make a new world'" (267).[304] As McKegney rightfully notes, "by initially failing to break out of the ideological system imposed upon them, the brothers are able to access the empowering capacity of traditional Cree thought."[305]

In their mutual theatrical engagement Jeremiah composes a play and Gabriel stages it. Jeremiah incorporates the myth of the Son of Ayash into his play. Therein Jeremiah processes his brother's past and writes: "'Remember, my son,' […] 'the way into the underworld of the human spirit is filled with danger, that you will meet evil men'" (278). For Gabriel's role he writes: "'No,' […] 'I am not the Son of Ayash'" (279). With this allusion, Jeremiah addresses Gabriel's participation in the joys of evil men. He implicitly reproaches Gabriel for his indulgence of entering into "the dark places of the human soul." For Jeremiah, the fact that his way is filled with danger becomes painfully apparent through Gabriel's suffering of AIDS. Jeremiah resents Gabriel for his failure to withstand the temptations of "the underworld of the human spirit," and the brothers wage a "cold war of thirteen years" (239). Thus he assigns him a role where he openly declares that he is not the Son of Ayash.

Jeremiah himself, however, identifies with the Son of Ayash in his creative adap-

---

[302] *Control*, 73.
[303] *Politics*, 96.
[304] *Control*, 73.
[305] *Politics*, 96.

tation of the myth. His self-identification with the hero of the myth is strengthened by his own history of early abandonment at residential school and the ordeals he was subjected to on the territory of the duplicitous Christianity. Jeremiah writes in his play: "*eehee, Ayash oogoosisa* had to go out into the world at a very young age" (274). Moreover, comparably to the Son of Ayash, who endeavours to fix the wounded world, Champion-Jeremiah attempts to reconstruct his by working "towards his own healing and that of the child."[306]

Furthermore, McKegney alleges that the separation part of the tale "speaks to Jeremiah's separation from … an essentially female Cree spiritual worldview by an invading patriarchal Christianity."[307] Since the Cree language has "no gender" (298), God can be represented by a woman in Cree religious spirituality. Highway explains that the trickster, called in Cree Weesageechak, is "as pivotal and important a figure" of North American Indian mythology "as Christ is the realm of Christian mythology."[308] The shape-shifting trickster can transcend time and "assume any guise he chooses."[309] The Fur Queen, a "goddess in fur" (298) is "a female trickster figure based primarily on the androgynous Cree trickster Weesageechak."[310] The Cree goddess in fur frequently appears throughout the novel. Highway elucidates that "without the continued presence of this extraordinary figure, the core of Indian culture would be gone forever."[311] In the novel, the Cree matriarchalism is mentioned in a reference to "the last shaman" Chachagathoo, who was "the last medicine woman [and] the last woman priest" (247) on Mistik Lake. She was accused of witchcraft by a Catholic priest and "sent to jail in Winnipeg" where, "in despair, she hung herself" (246). Thus Jeremiah identifies through the Son of Ayash myth his separation from home and from the traditional female spiritual worldview.

3.3.2 The Protagonists' Spiritual Homecoming

Highway depicts Gabriel's late realisation of the Weetigo of his past. Shortly before Gabriel dies of AIDS, he finally realises that "the true face of Father Lafleur is that of

---

[306] *Control*, 73.
[307] *Control*, 69.
[308] Highway, Tomson: *Kiss of the Fur Queen*. Norman: University of Oklahoma Press 2008, vii. Hereafter referred to as *Kiss*.
[309] *Kiss*, vii.
[310] *Return*, 160.
[311] *Kiss*, vii.

the evil Cree cannibal spirit, the Weetigo."[312] In Jeremiah's play *"Ulysses Thunder-child"* (277), the playwright assigns Gabriel "to direct it" (278) and to dance the lead role in it. The ill-stricken Gabriel adds a significant phrase to the script of the play: "But the cannibal spirit shedding his costume at death, revealing a priest's cassock, confuses the viewer" (285). The line reveals that Gabriel finally realises what Jeremiah realised when he saw Gabriel being molested by the priest. Additionally, shortly after the performance, tormented by a nightmare of his abuse, Gabriel replaces his original association of the rape in Christian spiritual terms with the evil spirit of the Weetigo. In a nightmare he sees the abusive priest and mumbles: "Haven't you feasted on enough human flesh?" (297).

In the final chapter of the novel, Highway depicts Gabriel's death in a hospital bedroom as a native spiritual homecoming. Shackleton emphasises that "Jeremiah 'comes home' to his cultural roots at the death bed of his brother."[313] Jeremiah "initiates the sweetgrass purification ceremonies of the Cree and slams the door in the Catholic priest's face."[314] Moreover, Highway alleviates the loss of his brother through Gabriel's final acknowledgement of the evil spirit in the face of his rapist and celebrates his return to the Native religion. The narrator illustrates Gabriel's explicit association of the priest with the Weetigo. Gabriel has a vision on his deathbed: "The Weetigo [comes] at Gabriel with his tongue lolling, its claws reaching for his groin" (299). Gabriel realises that "the cannibal spirit now ha[s] the face of Father Roland Lafleur" (300). He banishes "the creature ... brandishing a crucifix," and screams, "Get away from me" (300). Through Jeremiah's assistance in the conduction of the Cree religious ceremony, Gabriel's soul can be saved from hell. Jeremiah is relieved, "For God ha[s] finally come for his brother, banging on the door, demanding to be let in" (305). Highway can find consolation in the vision of the coming of the Fur Queen on Gabriel's deathbed, for at least shortly before Gabriel dies, he succeeds in finding his Indian self. After Gabriel passes away the Fur Queen "kisse[s] him. And [takes] him by the hand" (306).

Moreover, in the final scene of the novel, Highway draws a link between Gabriel's heavenly ascension and their father's famous story of the apparition of the Fur Queen after his winning of "the World Championship Dog Derby" (11) in 1951. Highway embeds the apparition of the goddess on Gabriel's deathbed into an analogical

---

[312] *Queen*, 91.
[313] *Return*, 160.
[314] *Return*, 160.

depiction of his father's vision of the Fur Queen. In Abraham's vision of the Cree goddess, the trickster appears disguised as the winner "of the 1951 Fur Queen Beauty Pageant" (8). Comparably, in Jeremiah's vision of the goddess, Weesageechak assumes the shape of "The Fur Queen, 1987" (306). According to Jeremiah's Cree way of making myths, "the Fur Queen [sweeps] into the room" and "lean[s] to Gabriel's cheek" (306). Strongly resembling Abraham's description, "the creature of unearthly beauty" (11, 306) floats towards Gabriel. Descending, the Fur Queen kisses Abraham's/Gabriel's "left cheek" (11, 306).

In addition to this, the traditional purification ceremony finally enables the Fur Queen to watch over Gabriel. His mother, Mariesis, says to the young Gabriel while she is packing his suitcase for residential school: "The Fur Queen will watch over you," and "The white fox on her cape will protect you from evil men" (74). Even though the goddess fails to save Gabriel from the evil forces during his lifetime, her care can be finally restored through the brothers' interaction at the level of their spiritual homecoming. As Shackleton stresses, "the ultimate finale comes when the Fur Queen ... take[s] Gabriel to his spiritual home."[315] Thus Highway concludes the novel with a successful restoration of his brother's Aboriginal religious spirituality: "Rising from the body, Gabriel Okimasis and the Fur Queen float [...] off into the swirling mist, as the little white fox on the collar of the cape turn[s] to Jeremiah. And wink[s]" (306).

With Jeremiah's successful appropriation of the Cree way of making myths, Highway describes a self-therapeutical strategy for coming to terms with the loss of his brother to the dangers of white men. As Shackleton rightly notes, the Fur Queen's "synecdochic symbol, the white fox fur, winks at Jeremiah, as if passing on a message of optimism in the face of catastrophe."[316] Through the trickster figure, Highway brings into his narrative what Gerald Vizenor calls "the imagination of tribal stories, and the power of tribal stories to heal. Stories that enlighten and relieve and relieve. Stories that create as they're being told. And stories that overturn the burdens of our human existence."[317] Therefore, the author validates Howells's assertion that "Native spiritual beliefs are shown to serve as survival strategies in the contemporary world."[318]

---

[315] *Return*, 160.
[316] *Return*, 161.
[317] *Politics*, 83.
[318] *Queen*, 91.

3.3.3. Towards an Individual and National Reconstruction

One of the goals of Highway's writing is a restoration of the lost identity and the indigenous belief system. It is a personal restoration of what was lost through the oppressive system of forced colonisation. The novel mirrors Jeremiah's struggle and the eventual success of the reappropriation of his Indian identity and cultural belonging. The trauma novel represents a retrospective effort to give meaning to the anguish endured beyond normal human experience. As Tal states, Highway's "process of storytelling [is] a personally reconstructive act."[319] By writing down his past, the victim can own it and gains control over it. In this way, he or she prevents the trauma from gaining control over him or her and directing the path of his or her life. Instead, he or she takes over the reins of his or her life.

In the novel, Jeremiah's day job in the Muskoosis Club of Ontario is to provide "urban Indian children ... with REC: recreation, education, culture" (269). Following Bhabha, "performing cultural identification, is the most effective means of achieving cultural identification."[320] In his terms, (pedagogy positions the colonized as an object). Bhabha equates the performative to the pedagogical. Bhabha's (notion of the performative is rooted in British language theorist J. L. Austin's influential work *How to Do Things With Words* (1962)). In Austin's understanding, (to issue an utterance (whether spoken or written) is to perform the action spoken). In a stretched sense of Austin's notion of the performative, it encompasses story, visual art, theory and theatrical performance as alternative forms of utterances.[321] Hence, Jeremiah's theatrical performances symbolise the pedagogical, for "the performance act forces the colonizers to gaze, because they cannot help but see/hear the performance."[322] With the play *Ulysses Thunderchild* Jeremiah employs his artistic creativity and creates "a site for enunciation and invention,"[323] thus enabling the cultural identification of his people. Howells argues that with the "dual incarnation as the 'Okimasis brothers'," Highway creates "the artist as a modern Cree culture warrior."[324]

Hogeterp-Koopman argues that in Bhabha's terms, "performative hybridity 'turn[s] the gaze of the discriminated back upon the eye of power' by illustrating the difference of the colonized, thereby providing a 'counter-narrative' to an essentialist

---

[319] *Hurt*, 121.
[320] *Trickster*, 198. All further references in the text are to this edition.
[321] Cp. *Trickster*, 198.
[322] *Trickster*, 199.
[323] *Trickster*, 198.
[324] *Queen*, 90.

national history."[325] In this sense, Highway's cultural hybridity enables him to compose a novel which "redirects the gaze of discrimination back into the eyes of power, [and] the redirected gaze must be acknowledged by the heirs of the colonizers."[326] Analogically, in the novel his protagonists compose plays of intercultural significance and put them on stage before a white Canadian audience.

The piece of literature is not only an elegy for his deceased brother and a tool for the restoration of his cultural identity but also a novel that has the capacity to build intercultural bridges. It is more than a critique and accusation for the stolen childhood. In the novel, Highway describes a process in which he generates "the creative weaponry to defeat the Weetigo of his past."[327] With this mythical weaponry Highway (inaugurates a new stage in the evolution of Residential School discourse). McKegney emphasises that the author of the novel (explores the 'meaning' of the Residential School experience) through politicised storytelling; namely by infusing history (with the very Cree spiritual dimension that Residential School sought to extinguish). He points out, (in this way he inverts the assimilation process). In his "extraordinarily political novel," Highway struggles to establish a "post-residential school Indigenous empowerment."[328] McKegney states that by speaking "directly to the limitations, in terms of Indigenous empowerment," Highway provides a "serious reconsideration of the unhealthy and distinctly non-Indigenous ideological basis of structures."[329]

It was not until 1998 that the Canadian government offered an official apology for the wrongs of the Residential School system.[330] Whether or not coincidentally published in the same year, *Kiss of the Fur Queen* "inaugurates a new stage in the evolution of Residential School discourse" in Canada.[331] McKegney notes that in John Milloy's terms the contemporary problem is that Aboriginal people are "now 'sick,' not savage, in need of psychological, rather than theological salvation."[332] With the novel, Highway unveils the residential school transgressions and confronts the government with its responsibility to deal with the effects. The novel's political tendency endorses the Indians' right for acceptance of their own position within the Canadian state.

In the first place, Highway composed the novel for Native readers. As he himself

---

[325] *Trickster*, 199.
[326] *Trickster*, 199.
[327] *Control*, 73. All further references in the text are to this edition.
[328] *Politics*, 103-4.
[329] *Politics*, 103.
[330] Cp. *Control*, 68.
[331] *Control*, 68.
[332] *Politics*, 84.

once stated, "I wrote [*Kiss of the Fur Queen*] for a Cree readership [...] I hope to reach the kids in the mall in Saskatoon and Winnipeg."[333] Thus, following Highway's intention, the novel "speaks with particular force to an Indigenous audience struggling to deal with the awful legacy of Canada's residential school system."[334] Therefore, the novel works towards a reinvigoration of tribal values in Indigenous communities living in Canada.[335] With *Kiss of the Fur Queen* Highway lays the foundations for the socio-political change necessary for the "newly conceived Indigenous empowerment outside the frameworks [...] of Euro-Canadian ideology and discourse."[336]

In the novel, Jeremiah shows resistance to the cultural obliteration of his people through his engagement with the cultural revival of Canada's First Nations. His mission is analogous to Fanon's appeal "in *The Wretched of the Earth*, considering the resistance to national cultures by postcolonial subjects."[337] There, Fanon states, "Each generation must, out of relative obscurity, discover its mission, fulfil it, or betray it."[338] Thus, quite in Fanon's sense, the "Cree-language revivalist" (270) discovers and fulfils his mission as a cultural revivalist of his ethnic community. Through the restitution of "the Cree way of telling stories, of making myth" (38), the author regains his cultural identity and finds his mission. As McKegney claims, Jeremiah's channelling of "his anguish into creative work" not only aids "his personal healing" but, in addition, provides "the cultural materials for a broader Indigenous empowerment."[339]

Moreover, Highway gives his critique a new significance, quite in Caruth's sense. She "insists on the ethical significance of this critical practice."[340] Caruth maintains that (the language of trauma, and the silence of its mute repetition of suffering) demand a (new mode of reading and listening). She suggests an alternative mode of reading trauma. According to Caruth, (trauma itself may provide the very link between cultures). Trauma forms (a bridge between disparate historical experiences), and (listening to the trauma of another can contribute to cross-cultural solidarity and to the creation of new forms of community). Like Highway, Jeremiah creates the world anew through narrative, not only for himself, but also for those who hear his stories. Highway transforms his horrible experience into a socially reconstructive act and takes up his respon-

---

333 *Politics*, 102.
334 *Politics*, 102.
335 Cp. *Politics*, 103.
336 *Politics*, 103.
337 *British*, 178.
338 *British*, 178.
339 *Politics*, 101.
340 *Studies*, 1. All further references in the text are to this edition.

sibility as a writer to induce a social and political change and to create an intercultural understanding that would "prevent the enactment of similar horrors in the future."[341]

With his engagement Highway-Jeremiah fulfils his political mission of cultural restoration and employs his creativity to build an intercultural bridge for reciprocal understanding. The novel reveals that "by first interpreting the world according to simulations of dominance, the brothers endanger their struggle against the adverse aftermath of childhood trauma"[342] but then redirect their worldview and resist the dominating power. Through the intercultural challenge of the highly self-reflexive testimony, Highway's traumatic experience assumes a transformation "from individual experience to the collective archive, from personal trauma to public memory."[343] The writer's intermingling cultures extend the lone purpose of criticising Canada's Christian churches. He establishes a connection between the oppressors and the oppressed. Highway's semi-omniscient narrator assumes the role of a Native translator throughout the novel and thus enables non-Native readers to comprehend the Cree spiritual system. By providing non-Native readers with an insight into Indian tribal values and spirituality, Highway establishes an intercultural exchange that goes beyond Native readership. Since knowledge about the Other is essential for the successful maintenance of an intercultural dialogue, the novel provides a unique possibility for non-Native readers to access and comprehend Indian otherness.

---

[341] *Hurt*, 121.
[342] *Politics*, 96.
[343] *Zimbabwe*, 2.

4. Conclusion

In the postcolonial novels *Nervous Conditions* and *Kiss of the Fur Queen* I have explored colonial and postcolonial identities. I have looked at the protagonists' culturally hybrid identities in a highly problematic living environment. The colonial condition, marked by oppression, acculturation, displacement, segregation and loss, places the colonised in a highly stressful environment. In their self-reflexive writings, the authors reveal the painful quest for identity with the inner and outer tensions caught between tradition and progress of the changing situation. The authors explore the construction, performance and shifts of self in interaction with their respective sentiments and situations. The main characters of the novels negotiate between their desire for the Other and the denial of native identity and tradition. Dangarembga and Highway depict the distressing process of the colonisation of the mind and, subsequently, their individual efforts for its decolonisation. I have investigated the ambivalent and multiple nature of colonised identities. The study has shown that a constant renegotiation and reconfiguration of self is intrinsic to all cultural hybrids in the process of colonisation. Being subjected to a series of traumatic experiences, the colonised must shape and reshape their worldview and therefore their identities. The societal and linguistic frameworks of antagonistic cultures additionally complicate identity formation. The novels have shown how the Western individualist ideology infects and annihilates the native sense of community and belonging. The study has confirmed that the multiple and shifting selves of the colonised stand in opposition to the essentialist perspective on identity, which assumes unity and closure. Focusing on identity less as being and more as becoming, the notion of cultural hybridity has expanded the traditional identity model. Therefore, the issue of hybrid identities has inspired a number of colonial theorists to disapprove of the standard identity model. The novels confirm the theories of the debate over cultural hybrids, "whose identity is its difference"[344] and defy the "antagonistic binarisms between the rulers and the ruled."[345] Bhabha's argument for the 'third space', an equivalent of the position in-between, provides an antithesis to the essentialist perspective. The main characters' mimicry of hegemonic authorities designate them as the mimic men of Bhabha's theories. My research concerning (post)colonial identities has revealed the multifaceted side of the self, and therefore has convinced me of the novels' validity for the anti-essentialist perspective.

---

[344] *Memory*, 7.
[345] *Migration*, 195.

Moreover, I have explored the impact of trauma on identity formation. The exposure to continuous stress complicates a smooth development of self. Traumatic events are beyond usual human experience and overthrow the victim's frame of reference of himself or herself and the world. Traumatic events force the traumatised to reconceptualise their understanding of the world and to readjust their identities to a new situation. Furthermore, I have explored the nature and impact of colonial trauma and the characters' reaction to the devastating experiences. The novels query the Western focus on single trauma and disclose instead the chronic nature of colonial trauma. As a result of living in a continuously stressful environment, the characters in the novels endure multiple traumatic experiences characteristic of colonialism. Consequently, they evolve certain behavioural patterns symptomatic of posttraumatic stress disorder (PTSD), a psychopathology resulting from traumatic experience. I have traced the symptoms of PTSD and hence confirmed the characters' intense suffering resulting from their traumas. They show several typical symptoms of PTSD. In addition, my research has confirmed the continuous nature of trauma on the side of the colonised and has invalidated the western-biased definition of PTSD as a reaction to a single horrific experience of trauma. The novels have portrayed that the "chronic psychic suffering" of colonial subjects is a product of "structural violence of racial, gender, sexual, class and other inequalities."[346] The findings have revealed a gap in the research of trauma studies in non-Western settings and call for a reconsideration of the terms.

I have compared critical essays on Fanon's writings to the novels and found therein analogies and differences. His work *Black Skin, White Masks* offers a good representation of ambiguity and the unbridgeable gaps in the attempt of the colonised to imitate their colonial masters. In The *Wretched of the Earth*, he depicts the violence inherent to colonialism represented in the novels. For the most part, the novels confirm Fanon's theories about the malign nature of colonialism and the psychological consequences on the side of the colonised. However, I have detected shortcomings in his theories, issues he left ignored or did not further elaborate. Dangarembga's novel explores the issues Fanon left ignored and therefore challenges his writings.

The analysis of *Nervous Conditions* has revealed the impact and effects of colonial trauma brought about by the British intrusion into the balance of the traditional Shona culture. The novel extends and challenges Fanon's writings by presenting the view of the colonised female native. It shows the additional burdens of double oppres-

---

[346] *Studies*, 3.

sion of native African women by colonialism and patriarchy. The author subdivides the nervousness of the novel's characters into gendered categories and gives native women a voice. The novel demonstrates the dangers of Westernisation to the harmony of communal and relational bonds. Moreover, Nyasha's bulimia/anorexia nervosa and Nhamo's death show the immediate destructive effects of colonisation. The novel identifies Westernisation by calling it "Englishness"—a socially deadly disease. The novelist depicts the impact of psychic trauma and presents a concrete example of the revolutionary consciousness necessary for resistance, left unelaborated by Fanon. She implies women's point of departure to generate resistance as better than that of men due to their greater distance from the colonial centre. The main character, Tambudzai, undergoes a complex path of identity formation and self-realisation with the help of her critique-laden anglicised cousin Nyasha. As a colonial hybrid, Tambu occupies Bhabha's 'third space'. Nyasha's deep cultural hybridity "is riven with the notion of 'ambivalence'" which exemplifies "the attraction-repulsion to colonial discourse."[347] Nyaha's anorexia or bulimia nervosa is an expression of the underlying deep social upheaval and presents her as the most endangered character of the novel. The novel shows objections to Western traditional thinking in binary oppositions and suggests that in a (post)colonial world, adding a new, third category, a position in-between, seems to be more appropriate. Consequently, the novelist buttresses her position and lets Tambu survive her trauma of gendered inequalities by letting her find her own way, a way between assimilation and tradition.

The analysis of *Kiss of the Fur Queen* has shown the sinister impact of physic and psychic traumas endured by two young Cree brothers on future lives. The novel has shown the difficulties of identity construction by addressing questions of cultural transgression, diaspora, translation, mimicry and denial. Early uprootedness and subjection to sexual abuse triggers the boys' trauma. Similar traumas haunt the brothers' lives but they take different paths in dealing with it. Whereas Gabriel's promiscuous homosexuality leads to his death from AIDS, Jeremiah resorts to the creative process of writing and explores his childhood trauma entwined in a mythic discourse. The novel has shown the supportive function of Indian myths and legends for the characters' comprehension of incomprehensible events, and my analysis of the novel has disclosed alternative approaches for dealing with trauma. It suggests that Western modes of trauma therapy are deficient and neglect Indigenous means of coping. Highway presents

---

[347] *Response*, 60.

a creative restoration of Indian culture on stage and page. He discovers the creative weaponry of Indian mythology to defeat the trauma of his past and heal the wounds of his soul. The Cree mythological embedding of the trauma narrative restores Jeremiah's/Highway's culture and alleviates his traumas. The Cree author accomplishes Fanon's appeal for resistance and finds his mission as a cultural revivalist. Therefore, the novel achieves a political function and contributes to the national empowerment of Canada's First Nations.

The characters in the novels develop their own strategies for coping and living with their traumatic experiences. Even though they are never able to restore the self to its previous state before the onset of colonisation, the characters succeed in finding a solution, a reconciliatory path, for coping with their traumas. Both main protagonists, Tambudzai and Jeremiah, draw strength from their culture and the acknowledgement of their ancestry. They find a way to resist the forces of colonial authorities, reconstruct and decolonise their minds, and draw their own advantages from colonial education. The semi-autobiographical novels show that the authors have appropriated colonial education to redirect the gaze of the formerly colonised back upon the eye of power. Moreover, the novels give voice to the formerly oppressed and silenced individuals and offer a precious opportunity for non-native readers to comprehend the Other. With the novels, Highway and Dangarembga not only criticise the former colonial regimes of their respective countries but also contribute to the intercultural dialogue between the former centre of power and its peripheries. Therefore, with the novels they build bridges for cross-cultural understanding.

The study of the novels *Nervous Conditions* and *Kiss of the Fur* Queen has un-veiled the gaps of trauma studies and asks for a revision of the Western-biased approach to trauma. Postcolonial literatures enable an insight into alternative approaches for dealing with and accommodating trauma. The literatures provide a point of departure for a cross-cultural conception of trauma. I am interested in the indigenous means for coping with traumatic experiences which might be reverse-applied to the West. What has the Western trauma research still to learn about trauma from the long-ignored indigenous peoples? In a multicultural, postcolonial world an inclusion of different modes of healing trauma seems to be necessary, and its understanding can be drawn, amongst other sources, from literature.

Works Cited

Antze, Paul et al. (ed.): *Tense Past: Cultural Essays in Trauma and Memory*. New York: Routledge 1996.

Athabasca University. 2011. "Tomson Highway." *English-Canadian Writers*. <http://www.athabascau.ca/cll/writers/english/writers/thighway/thighway.php> (03.06.2012).

Bak, Hans: "The City as a Site of Trauma and Transformation: Sherman Alexie's 'Indian Killer' and Tomson Highway's 'Kiss of the Fur Queen'." *Anglophonia: French Journal of English Studies*, 25 (2009).

Bower, Gordon H., Heidi Sivers: "Cognitive Impact of Traumatic Events." *Development and Psychopathology: Risk, Trauma, Memory*, 10.4 (1998).

Brown, Laura S.: "Not Outside the Range: One Feminist Perspective on Psychic Trauma." In Cathy Caruth (ed.): *Trauma: Explorations in Memory*. Baltimore: John Hopkins University Press 1995.

Buelens, Gert, Steff Craps: "Introduction: Postcolonial Trauma Novels." *Studies in the Novel*, 40, 1,2 (2008).

Caruth, Cathy (ed.): *Trauma: Explorations in Memory*. Baltimore: John Hopkins University Press 1995.

: *Unclaimed Experience: Trauma, Narrative, and History*. Baltimore: John Hopkins University Press 1996.

Counihan, Clare: "Reading the Figure of Woman in African Literature: Psychoanalysis, Difference, and Desire." *Research in African Literatures*, 38.2 (2007).

Dangarembga, Tsitsi: *Nervous Conditions*. Banbury: Ayebia Clarke Publishing Ltd. 2004.

Di Prete, Laura: *Foreign Bodies: Trauma, Corporeality and Textuality in Contemporary American Culture*. New York: Routledge 2006.

Edwards, Justin D.: *Postcolonial Literature*. Basingstoke: Palgrave Macmillan 2008.

Eslamieh, Salumeh: "Tsitsi Dangarembga's 'Nervous Conditions': Coming of Age and Adolescence as Representative of Multinational Hybridity." *Moveable Type: Childhood and Adolescence*, 1.1 (2005). <http://www.ucl.ac.uk/english/graduate/issue/1_1/salumeh.htm> (04.11.2011).

Erikson, Kai: "Notes on Trauma and Community." In: Cathy Caruth (ed.): *Trauma: Explorations in Memory*. Baltimore: John Hopkins University Press 1995.

Fagan, Kristina: Weesageechak Meets the Weetigo: Storytelling, Humour, and Trauma in the Fiction of Richard Van Camp, Tomson Highway, and Eden Robinson. *Studies in Canadian Literature*, 34.1 (2009).

Gandhi, Leela: *Postcolonial Theory, a Critical Introduction*. Edinburgh: Edinburgh University Press 1998.

Ghadi, Alirza Sadegh: *Cultural Translation And Post Colonialism*. <http://www.articlesnatch.com/Article/Cultural-Translation-And-Post-Colonialism/513892#ixzz1RWDQL6lw> (03.05.2012).

Godiwala, Dimple: "Response to Homi Bhabha's Theory of 'Mimicry'." In: Joel Kuortti et al.: *Reconstructing Hybridity: Postcolonial Studies in Transition*. Amsterdam: Rodopi 2007.

Granofsky, Ronald: *The Trauma Novel: Contemporary Symbolic Depictions of Collective Disaster*. New York: Lang 1995.

Hawley, John C.: "Tsitsi Dangarembga's Ambiguous Adventure: Nervous Conditions and the Blandishments of Mission Education." In: Gerhard Stilz (ed.): *Missions of Interdependence. A Literary Directory*. Amsterdam: Rodopi 2002.

Highway, Tomson: *Kiss of the Fur Queen*. Norman: University of Oklahoma Press 2008.

Hogeterp-Koopman, Jane: "Bhabha, the Trickster and the Church: Re-viewing Canda's Post-Colonial Present." In: Deborah E. Bowen (ed.): *The Strategic Smorgasbord of Postmodernity: Literature and the Christian Critic*. Newcastle: Cambridge Scholars Publishing 2007.

Howells, Coral Ann: "Tomson Highway: 'Kiss of the Fur Queen'." In: Coral Ann Howells (ed.): *Where are the Voices Coming From? Canadian Culture and the Legacies of History*. Amsterdam: Rodopi 2004.

Ikas, Karin, Gerhard Wagner (ed.): "Communicating in the Third Space." *Transnational Literature*, 3.1 (2010). <http://dspace.flinders.edu.au/jspui/bitstream/2328/15136/1/Communicating%20in%20the%20third%20space.pdf> (17.6.2012).

Kagee, Ashraf: "Testing the DSM Model in South Africa." In: Ewald Mengel (ed.): *Trauma, Memory, and Narrative in South Africa: Interviews*. Amsterdam: Rodopi 2010.

King, Bruce (ed.): *New National and Post-Colonial Literatures*: *An Introduction*. Oxford: Clarendon Press 1998.

Klein, Verena: "Healing the Native Canadian Soul: Three Accounts of Spiritual Homecoming." *Litteraria Pragensia: Studies in Literature and Culture*, 15.30 (2005).

Kunow, Rüdiger, Wilfred Raussert (ed.): *Cultural Memory and Multiple Identities*. Berlin: Lit 2008.

Loomba, Ania: *Colonialism, Postcolonialism*. London: Routledge 1998.
: *Colonialism, Postcolonialism*. London: Routledge 2002.

Luckhurst, Roger: *The Trauma Question*. London: Routledge 2008.

McKegney, Sam: "Claiming Narrative Control: Tomson Highway on Residential Schooling." *Culture and the State: Disability Studies & Indigenous Studies,* 2003.
: "From Trickster Poetics to Transgressive Politics." *Studies in American Indian Literatures*, 17.4 (2005).

Murray, Jessica: A post-colonial and feminist reading of selected testimonies to trauma in post-liberation South Africa and Zimbabwe. *Journal of African Cultural Studies*, 21.1 (2009).

Nair, Supriya: "Melancholic Women – The Intellectual Hysteric(s) in Nervous Conditions." *Research in African Literatures*, 26.2 (1995).

Papastergiadis, Nikos: *The Turbulence of Migration: Globalization, Deterritorialization and Hybridity*. Oxford: Polity Press 2007.

Pristed, Helene: "The Concept of Identity." In: Wojciech H. Kalaga et al. (ed.): *Multicultural Dilemmas: Identity, Difference, Otherness*. Frankfurt am Main: Lang 2008.

Rothberg, Michael: "Decolonizing Trauma Studies: A Response." *Studies in the Novel*, 40.1,2 (2008).

Scahatteman, Renee: *Fanon and Beyond: The 'Nervous Condition' of the Colonized Woman*. In: Kofi Anyidoho et al. (ed.): Beyond Survival: African Literatures & the Search for New Life. Trenton: Africa World Press 1998.

Shackleton, Mark: "The Return of the Native American: The Theme of Homecoming in Contemporary Native North American Fiction." *The Atlantic Literary Review*, 3.2 (2002).

Sizemore, Christine W.: "Negotiating Between Ideologies: The Search for Identity in Tsitsi Dangarembga's 'Nervous Conditions' and Margret Atwood's 'Cat's Eye'." *Women's Studies Quarterly*, 25.3/4 (1997).

Sugnet, Charles: "'Nervous Conditions': Dangarembga's Feminist Reinvention of Fanon." In: Obioma Nnaemeka (ed.): *The Politics of (M)Othering*. London: Routledge 1997.

Tal, Kali: *Worlds of Hurt: Reading the Literatures of Trauma*. Cambridge: Cambridge University Press 1996.

Tew, Philip: *Contemporary British Novel*. London: Continuum 2004.

Thomas, Sue: "Killing the Hysteric in the Colonized's House: Tsitsi Dangarembga's 'Nervous Conditions'." *The Journal of Commonwealth Literature*, 27,1 (1992).

Vickroy, Laurie: *Trauma and Survival in Contemporary Fiction*. Charlottesville: University of Virginia Press 2002.

Wachinger, Tobias A.: *Posing In-Between: Postcolonial Englishness and the Commodification of Hybridity*. Frankfurt am Main: Lang 2003.

Zwicker, Heather: "The Nervous Collusions of Nation and Gender: Tsitsi Dangarembga's Challenge to Fanon." In: Treiber Jeanette et al. (ed.): *Negotiating the Postcolonial: Emerging Perspectives on Tsitsi Dangarembga*. Trenton: Africa World Press 2002.

List of Abbreviations

Adolescence   Eslamieh, Salumeh: "Tsitsi Dangarembga's 'Nervous Conditions':
Coming of Age and Adolescence as Representative of Multinational
Hybridity." *Moveable Type: Childhood and Adolescence*, 1.1 (2005).
<http://www.ucl.ac.uk/english/graduate/issue/1_1/salumeh.htm>
(04.11.2011).

Adventure   Hawley, John C.: "Tsitsi Dangarembga's Ambiguous Adventure:
Nervous Conditions and the Blandishments of Mission Education." In:
Gerhard Stilz (ed.): *Missions of Interdependence. A Literary Direc-
tory.* Amsterdam: Rodopi 2002.

Beyond   Scahatteman, Renee: *Fanon and Beyond: The 'Nervous Condition' of
the Colonized Woman.* In: Kofi Anyidoho et al. (ed.): Beyond Survival: African Literatures & the Search for New Life. Trenton: Africa
World Press 1998.

Bodies   Di Prete, Laura: *Foreign Bodies: Trauma, Corporeality and Textuality
in Contemporary American Culture.* New York: Routledge 2006.

British   Tew, Philip: *Contemporary British Novel.* London: Continuum 2004.

City   Bak, Hans: "The City as a Site of Trauma and Transformation:
Sherman Alexie's 'Indian Killer' and Tomson Highway's 'Kiss of the
Fur Queen'." *Anglophonia: French Journal of English Studies*, 25
(2009).

Cognitive   Bower, Gordon H., Heidi Sivers: "Cognitive Impact of Traumatic
Events." *Development and Psychopathology: Risk, Trauma, Memory*,
10.4 (1998).

Collusions   Zwicker, Heather: "The Nervous Collusions of Nation and Gender:
Tsitsi Dangarembga's Challenge to Fanon." In: Treiber Jeanette et al.
(ed.): *Negotiating the Postcolonial: Emerging Perspectives on Tsitsi
Dangarembga.* Trenton: Africa World Press 2002.

Colonialism   Loomba, Ania: Colonialism, Postcolonialism. London: Routledge
2002.

Community   Erikson, Kai: "Notes on Trauma and Community." In: Cathy Caruth
(ed.): *Trauma: Explorations in Memory.* Baltimore: John Hopkins
University Press 1995.

Control   McKegney, Sam: "Claiming Narrative Control: Tomson Highway on
Residential Schooling." *Culture and the State: Disability Studies &
Indigenous Studies,* 2003.

Decolonizing   Rothberg, Michael: "Decolonizing Trauma Studies: A Response."
Studies in the Novel, 40.1,2 (2008).

Homecoming   Klein, Verena: "Healing the Native Canadian Soul: Three Accounts of
Spiritual Homecoming." *Litteraria Pragensia: Studies in Literature
and Culture*, 15.30 (2005).

Hurt   Tal, Kali: *Worlds of Hurt: Reading the Literatures of Trauma.*
Cambridge: Cambridge University Press 1996.

Hysteric   Thomas, Sue: "Killing the Hysteric in the Colonized's House: Tsitsi
Dangarembga's 'Nervous Conditions'." *The Journal of Commonwealth Literature*, 27,1 (1992).

In-Between   Wachinger, Tobias A.: *Posing In-Between: Postcolonial Englishness
and the Commodification of Hybridity.* Frankfurt am Main: Lang
2003.

Kiss   Highway, Tomson: *Kiss of the Fur Queen*. Norman: University of
              Oklahoma Press 2008.
Literature   Edwards, Justin D.: *Postcolonial Literature*. Basingstoke: Palgrave
              Macmillan 2008.
Memory   Kunow, Rüdiger, Wilfred Raussert (ed.): *Cultural Memory and
              Multiple Identities*. Berlin: Lit 2008.
Migration   Papastergiadis, Nikos: *The Turbulence of Migration: Globalization,
              Deterritorialization and Hybridity*. Oxford: Polity Press 2007.
National   King, Bruce (ed.): *New National and Post-Colonial Literatures*: *An
              Introduction*. Oxford: Clarendon Press 1998.
Question   Luckhurst, Roger: The Trauma Question. London: Routledge 2008.
Negotiating   Sizemore, Christine W.: "Negotiating Between Ideologies: The Search
              for Identity in Tsitsi Dangarembga's 'Nervous Conditions' and Mar-
              gret Atwood's 'Cat's Eye'." *Women's Studies Quarterly*, 25.3/4
              (1997).
Novel   Granofsky, Ronald: *The Trauma Novel: Contemporary Symbolic
              Depictions of Collective Disaster*. New York: Lang 1995.
Politics   McKegney, Sam: "From Trickster Poetics to Transgressive Politics."
              Studies in American Indian Literatures, 17.4 (2005).
Postcolonialism Loomba, Ania: *Colonialism, Postcolonialism*. London: Routledge
              1998.
Queen   Howells, Coral Ann: "Tomson Highway: 'Kiss of the Fur Queen'." In:
              Coral Ann Howells (ed.): *Where are the Voices Coming From? Cana-
              dian Culture and the Legacies of History*. Amsterdam: Rodopi 2004.
Question   Luckhurst, Roger: *The Trauma Question*. London: Routledge 2008.
Reinvention   Sugnet, Charles: "'Nervous Conditions': Dangarembga's Feminist
              Reinvention of Fanon." In: Obioma Nnaemeka (ed.): *The Politics of
              (M)Othering*. London: Routledge 1997.
Response   Godiwala, Dimple: "Response to Homi Bhabha's Theory of 'Mim-
              icry'." In: Joel Kuortti et al.: *Reconstructing Hybridity: Postcolonial
              Studies in Transition*. Amsterdam: Rodopi 2007.
Return   Shackleton, Mark: "The Return of the Native American: The Theme
              of Homecoming in Contemporary Native North American Fiction."
              The Atlantic Literary Review, 3.2 (2002).
Space   Ikas, Karin, Gerhard Wagner (ed.): "Communicating in the Third
              Space." *Transnational Literature*, 3.1 (2010).
              <http://dspace.flinders.edu.au/jspui/bitstream/2328/15136/1/Communi
              cating%20in%20the%20third%20space.pdf> (17.6.2012).
Studies   Buelens, Gert, Steff Craps: "Introduction: Postcolonial Trauma
              Novels." *Studies in the Novel*, 40, 1,2 (2008).
Survival   Vickroy, Laurie: *Trauma and Survival in Contemporary Fiction*.
              Charlottesville: University of Virginia Press 2002.
Tense   Antze, Paul et al. (ed.): *Tense Past: Cultural Essays in Trauma and
              Memory*. New York: Routledge 1996.
Testing   Kagee, Ashraf: "Testing the DSM Model in South Africa." In: Ewald
              Mengel (ed.): *Trauma, Memory, and Narrative in South Africa: Inter-
              views*. Amsterdam: Rodopi 2010.
Theory   Gandhi, Leela: *Postcolonial Theory, a Critical Introduction*. Edin-
              burgh: Edinburgh University Press 1998.
Translation   Ghadi, Alirza Sadegh: *Cultural Translation And Post Colonialism*.

	<http://www.articlesnatch.com/Article/Cultural-Translation-And-Post-Colonialism/513892#ixzz1RWDQL6lw> (03.05.2012).
Trauma	Caruth, Cathy (ed.): *Trauma: Explorations in Memory*. Baltimore: John Hopkins University Press 1995.
Trickster	Hogeterp-Koopman, Jane: "Bhabha, the Trickster and the Church: Reviewing Canda's Post-Colonial Present." In: Deborah E. Bowen (ed.): *The Strategic Smorgasbord of Postmodernity: Literature and the Christian Critic*. Newcastle: Cambridge Scholars Publishing 2007.
Unclaimed	Caruth, Cathy: *Unclaimed Experience: Trauma, Narrative, and History*. Baltimore: John Hopkins University Press 1996.
Weesageechak	Fagan, Kristina: Weesageechak Meets the Weetigo: Storytelling, Humour, and Trauma in the Fiction of Richard Van Camp, Tomson Highway, and Eden Robinson. *Studies in Canadian Literature*, 34.1 (2009).
Writers	Athabasca University. 2011. "Tomson Highway." *English-Canadian Writers*. <http://www.athabascau.ca/cll/writers/english/writers/thighway/thighway.php> (03.06.2012).
Zimbabwe	Murray, Jessica: A post-colonial and feminist reading of selected testimonies to trauma in post-liberation South Africa and Zimbabwe. *Journal of African Cultural Studies*, 21.1 (2009).